PADDLENORTH

PADDLE

NORTH

ADVENTURE, RESILIENCE, AND RENEWAL IN THE ARCTIC WILD

JENNIFER KINGSLEY

David Suzuki Foundation

GREYSTONE BOOKS

VANCOUVER/BERKELEY

Greystone Books Ltd.
www.greystonebooks.com

David Suzuki Foundation
219–2211 West 4th Avenue
Vancouver BC Canada V6K 4S2

Cataloguing data available from Library and Archives Canada
ISBN 978-1-77164-177-7 (pbk.)
ISBN 978-1-77164-036-7 (epub)

Editing by Nancy Flight
Copy editing by Jennifer Croll
Cover design by Ingrid Paulson and Nayeli Jimenez
Text design by Ingrid Paulson
Cover photograph by Jennifer Kingsley
Photographs by Drew Gulyas, Tim Irvin, Jennifer Kingsley, and Levi Waldron
Title page photo: Paddling one of the Back's many lakes. Credit: Tim Irvin
Printed and bound in Canada by Friesens
Distributed in the U.S. by Publishers Group West

Canadä

We gratefully acknowledge the support of the Canada Council for the Arts,
the British Columbia Arts Council, the Province of British Columbia through the
Book Publishing Tax Credit, and the Government of Canada through the
Canada Book Fund for our publishing activities.

Greystone Books is committed to reducing the consumption of old-growth forests
in the books it publishes. This book is one step toward that goal.

for Tim

For some of us, wilderness is a place—maybe a park. For others, it's the essence of wild nature, and a park could never enclose it. Some call wilderness a cathedral; others call it a construction.

Inside wilderness lives the elusive idea of wildness, a shape-shifter that crawls onto the crease of a leaf, sleeps between skyscrapers, spreads across a mountain range, or rests in a drop of seawater. We could call it the spirit of wilderness, but wilderness cannot contain it. Wildness overflows the boundaries of location, refusing to conform to a scale or definition.

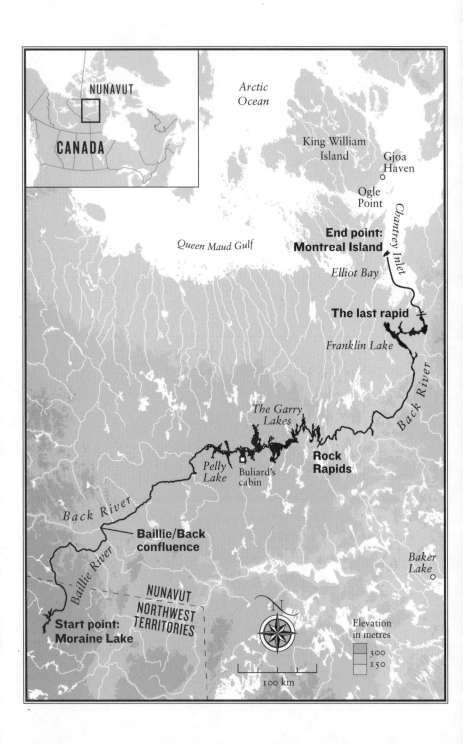

CONTENTS

CHAPTER 1

TO BEGIN, TO BEGIN

I climbed the thin steps of the Twin Otter floatplane carefully; it wouldn't do to twist an ankle before take-off. I squeezed by our stack of canoes and slid into a cold metal seat. As we taxied out into the bay and accelerated, the plane's vibrations became a steady roar. I reached for the company-issued earmuffs and prepared to be pushed back in my chair as we nosed upward. The plane dragged the heels of its pontoons along the water, and suddenly we were airborne.

I was surrounded by camping gear, fifty days' worth of food, and my five companions. Yellowknife disappeared within moments, along with the silver edge of Great Slave Lake. Ponds and small lakes stared blackly upward, and golden muskeg glowed between spruce trees. The horizon arced in the distance, and I wanted to believe that wilderness would not be broken again as we headed north. I stared at the ground, looking for animals, and my eyes were rewarded, not with moose or caribou, but with a paved road that gave way to gravel, and finally to the open pit of a diamond mine. The land was big enough to swallow hundreds of thousands of caribou, powerful rivers, and fresh scars of industry. I was used to studying the landscape from the black and white lines of topographical maps—most of which are too old to show the territories' newer faces.

Despite my nervousness and excitement, the howl of the airplane, and the cold that crept through its metal shell, I slumped against the wall and slept. Preparing for the trip had exhausted all of us. While I napped, we continued north, and the trees thinned out into isolated clumps and then disappeared altogether. I awoke to find Drew with his forehead pressed to the window, his eyes open wide in amazement. We had reached the tundra in springtime; no trees, but lots of ice. We were only the third group of paddlers to be dropped off by the air charter company so far that summer. All of the lakes, about half the surface of the land, flared white under the clouds. The ground resembled a muted painter's palette of grays, browns, and yellows mixed between bright patches of snow. No recognizable landforms stood out, no movement. Pools of color stretched to the curve of the earth.

Our planned landing was impossible; only a few sections of river were unfrozen. Tim wrestled with the map and pointed. The pilot nodded; the plane dipped left and spiraled down, its nose seeking water below. My view alternated from land to sky, land to sky, unsettling the lunch in my belly. The wings finally stabilized, but ice still zoomed under our feet. I felt the river before I saw it. We stuttered across its surface.

The Baillie River wears a trough into the tundra's rocky plain. This tributary would lead our group of six to the Back River, a massive 1,000-kilometer-long waterway that drains the central mainland of Nunavut, Canada's largest and northernmost territory. The Back boasts over eighty sets of rapids, 10-foot standing waves, boiling chutes, and an enormous system of lakes. We planned to spend fifty days winding our way to the Arctic Ocean. And it would all start here. My feet froze in the water as I carried a pack to shore. The river was only about 25 meters across.

The plane buzzed overhead and dipped its wings in farewell. I stood at the water's edge in a thin yellow windbreaker I wouldn't wear again for the rest of the trip, and scanned our heap of gear: three boats, three personal packs, four food packs, four food barrels (hip height, waterproof, and made from blue plastic), two wannigans (voyageur-style wooden boxes with removable lids and tumplines for carrying), and a mess of paddles, PFDs (personal flotation devices, aka life jackets), helmets, and day packs. Gusts of wind pulled at my hair and found the gap above my waistband. The painter's palette had sprung into a relief of small rises, but without trees or familiar landmarks, scale was hard to figure out.

We stood around feeling stunned by our new reality— we had been eating take-out noodles in Yellowknife three hours earlier—until Levi checked his thermometer and broke the silence. "It's only one degree," he said. "And how about that windchill?"

We scattered after that.

Alie sat down; Drew and Jen walked away from the water, picking up stones; Levi looked up at the sky; Tim walked the farthest. I stood by the river and cast my mind back three years to the first time I had set foot on the tundra. *Is this what I remember?* That summer lived in my memory

Arrival on the Baillie River. Left to right: Levi Waldron, Tim Irvin, Jenny Kingsley, Drew Gulyas, Jen McKay, Alie Pick. CREDIT: TIM IRVIN

as a sunny, buggy adventure filled with laughter and the good kind of challenge. It occurred to me that it might not be the same this time.

We came back together eventually, and Tim showed me the handful of soft brown qiviut, the underfur from a muskox, that he had found on the ground. He tucked it into a pocket and set up the camera for a picture. The six of us stood close together with our arms entwined. We smiled with pale faces, short hair, new pants, and clean shoes. We stared straight at the lens, our feet planted squarely on the tundra—except my right foot and Alie's left, which rolled out as if the ground were too hot or cold to stand on. Levi had a dark bandana wrapped around his black hair, and his Leatherman Multi-Tool hung from his belt. Tim draped an arm around Levi's shoulder and smiled broadly from under a baseball cap. Drew and I stood in the middle, freshly washed and confident, no hats. My dark hair barely curled behind my ears; his orange mop was cropped to a frizzy brush cut. Sunglasses held back Jen's blonde hair—like she was having a day at the beach—and she wrapped her arm around Alie, whose red fleece looked fresh off the rack.

The tundra filled in all around us. We stood on coarse, beige sand littered with fist- and skull-sized rocks. Each one was a different color—gray, black, purple, pink—and each was tattooed with splotches of lichen. Green and brown vegetation darkened the background, next to a small lake, and the horizon line cut behind us at waist level. Above it all, the clouds seemed to spread from a single point. They papered the sky white.

✴

THAT FIRST AFTERNOON was a blur of moving bags and searching for gear. We decided not to travel, or cook, until the next morning; the noodles would suffice until we slept.

Tim and I shared a tent the first night, but he didn't say much. I think he saved his energy for the group during those early days. He lay down with his back to me and started sleep-breathing within minutes. I had always envied his ability to fall asleep anywhere, anytime.

I slid off my outer clothes and climbed into the pouf of my sleeping bag. It smelled moist. My clammy feet stuck to the nylon. I lay back and waited for my body heat to generate a warm shell. I had no idea what time it was. Our tents crouched on the sand, 2 degrees south of the Arctic Circle, four days after the summer solstice. The sun would dip below the horizon for about three hours.

Silence filled the evening. The wind wasn't strong enough to make noise or push the tents around. I strained to hear something outside, but I couldn't. Not even the whine of a mosquito; it was still too cold for them. Tim's breathing, the odd rustle of nylon from the vestibule, every movement of my sleeping bag, and the sound of my legs shifting against my Therm-a-Rest completed the soundtrack.

I pulled out my journal and flipped through it in the beige light of the tent.

The first sixty-one pages were already covered with calculations and lists dating back six months to January 2005. Everything from food weights to diagrams of eddy turns to expenses and endless food shopping lists. Some items were cryptic: *ask about trip wire, write note about molasses.* Others were small but important: *go to dentist, ask group about toilet paper preferences.*

The lists became more scattered and more detailed as our departure day approached. Anything that I didn't write down I risked forgetting: *email about sunglasses, extra sugar and cinnamon.* I knew it was silly to pack all these lists across the tundra, but I wanted one book that would tell my story from the beginning to the end.

I wrote little about the details of that first day. I was more concerned about the feeling of being back on the tundra. Did I feel comfortable? Would I fit in with the group? What about Tim? I slept fitfully, haunted by a bird's-eye view of the landscape, with the camera pulling back. Our camp got smaller and smaller until we faded away completely.

✳

THE NEXT MORNING I stretched outside the tent and appraised my surroundings. I had arrived in the world's coldest biome. The Arctic tundra (there is also an alpine variety) is defined by relatively unappealing characteristics: year-round cold; lack of trees; permanently frozen ground, called permafrost, which leads to poorly drained soil; a short growing season; and low biodiversity. It's hardly travel bro-chure material, and its other names, the Barrenlands or simply the Barrens, don't inspire typical vacation dreams either. However, if you want to measure yourself against the Earth—to test your perspective on life and distance—there is nowhere better. Our planet is about 10 percent tundra, but relatively few of us will ever set foot on it. You can travel for weeks without finding another person, and what it lacks in diversity it makes up for in abundance. Millions of birds seek the Arctic tundra each spring; some, like the Arctic tern, fly all the way from South America to feed and breed. Legendary caribou migrations crisscross the tundra's surface, and equally renowned swarms of biting flies fill the summer air. Animals that stay year-round—like muskox and gyrfal-cons—push the limits of survival. It is one of the last places on Earth where apex predators like bears and wolves can live without much human interference. It is unlike anywhere else, and that is a wonder in itself, but in the three years since my last visit, I had forgotten about the tundra's oppressive moods. The landscape is so open—yet when the wind rises, the temperature drops, and the sky fills with clouds, the atmosphere becomes heavy, and you feel trapped by all that freedom. Around our camp, Labrador tea, dwarf birch, and willow—still brown from the weight of winter—rolled away in every direction. The richness of warming earth reached my nose but was knocked away by the steel smell of ice.

Morning brought our group's first point of order.

"Will today be the first day of the trip because it's our first full day out here?" asked Jen.

"I started the group journal last night with Day One," said Drew.

"Maybe today should be Day One and yesterday could be Day Zero because we didn't paddle anywhere," Alie offered.

"Or yesterday could be Day One and today is Day Two," said Levi.

"Today is Day One," Drew replied, "Day Two in New-foundland."

After bowls of granola with milk powder (coconut milk powder for Levi, who was vegan), we started to set up our partnerships. We decided not to establish fixed tent mates; if we rotated tent partners, we would get more one-on-one time with each other over the summer. We would have cooking partners to develop efficiency in the kitchen, but we could decide on those later. The most important thing to organize first was paddling partners. We needed to balance our skills to maximize safety. Choosing who would paddle with whom through the white water and big winds (we could switch up on the easier days) was like picking teams in gym class; it's best if the teams are even, but everybody wants to be on a good team. We paired Levi, an experienced paddler and a good teacher, with Jen, our least experienced paddler. Tim, another white-water vet, paddled with Alie, an experienced tripper with less white-water experience.

That left Drew, who spoke confidently about his white-water proficiency, and me, strong but out of practice. We planned to alternate between the bow and stern.

It's difficult to build a team of six people who can spend an entire summer far from home—especially when the team needs river skills, wilderness experience, a good balance of personalities, and, hopefully, a shared sense of humor. Our group was born the previous January when Tim and I pulled out a map of the Arctic. Tim was my closest friend, and over our ten-year friendship we had paddled at least a hundred days together. With the map spread out on the floor, we called Levi, our old canoe-tripping friend, who was finishing a PhD in wood science at the University of Toronto. He was an easy sell. Over the following weeks we combed our community for three more willing candidates. Drew had recently married, bought a house in Toronto, and left his job as the co-director of a summer camp for children with cancer. He wanted this once-in-a-lifetime adventure before returning to school for a master's in education, and later becoming a father. Alie was a writer working on both a poetry collection and a master's of philosophy in Newfoundland while awaiting the release of her first novel. She had completed two long canoe trips in the past and wanted a break before resuming life as an author. For Jen, this trip would be the perfect addition to a two-year leave of absence from the Ontario Ministry of the Environment, which she was spending in Yellowknife on a work transfer. It would also be a big change from her shorter outings on Ontario's lakes.

Before the expedition, we had various degrees of social interaction. Levi, Tim, and I were good friends already and had tested our compatibility on a previous Arctic trip. Jen and I had close friends in common but hadn't made the leap to one-on-one friendship ourselves. Drew and Alie were more like acquaintances to me (and to Tim), but I looked forward to knowing them better. As for the others, Drew and Jen were already buddies; they had known each other almost ten years. Both of them had paddled with Levi before. Alie was the bravest; she didn't have a good friend in the group yet, but she seemed so comfortable I never thought about that until later in the summer.

Before the trip we had all been socially connected, but soon we would become a society of our own.

* * *

MY FINGERS SWELLED from the cold as Drew and I heaved a barrel, personal pack, canoe pack, and wannigan into our boat: 300 pounds in all. I secured our throw bag (a small sack filled with loosely packed rope that can be thrown to a distressed swimmer) behind the stern seat and tied painters (ropes for tying up or towing a boat) to the bow and stern. We unrolled the spray deck that would attach to the hull and cover everything. It would help to keep us warm and dry through the rapids and wind, but I could hardly feel its tough nylon as we tugged the deck into position. I blew on my hands and climbed into the stern.

"Okay, let's go," I said.

Drew jumped in, and we pushed away from shore with the butts of our paddles. The river picked us up and carried us around the first bend. From shore, the water had looked black, but now I could see pebbles at the bottom. My arms sank into the pace of the paddle. I watched Drew to follow his rhythm. I kept my lower arm straight and led with my wrist. Both of my shoulders swiveled with the recovery of the stroke, and I used my core muscles to propel us forward. After twenty minutes, I started to warm up. Blood returned to my hands; my joints felt smooth, if a little weak. The pain would come later. It was still a long time before lunch.

It took a couple of hours to reach the ice. Giant blocks, 6 feet high and 20 across, littered the riverbanks by the hundreds, heaved up and broken by the spring thaw. The river flowed swiftly but remained narrow and shallow. We wound our way downstream, surrounded by towers of beached candle ice—each block a matrix of long vertical shards. On our first break, Jen and Drew ran over to the ice and gave it a swift kick. Icicles crashed toward them with the boom of a chandelier cut loose from a ballroom ceiling. Icy spikes encased their ankles. Alie and Levi climbed out of their boat to explore, and Tim and I followed. We kicked at the melting ice and chased each other between the towers with spears of glass while the tundra squelched beneath our boots. The sky remained overcast and settled on my shoulders.

Back on the river, we encountered our first riffles of fast water. We pulled on our helmets and practiced our paddle signals: "Go left," "Go right," "Okay?" and "Stop." The ice began to follow us later that day. Transparent growlers, small pieces of ice detached from the larger freshwater bergs, rode the current without making a sound. We started twirling our paddles over our heads, like majorettes, to warn each other about them. We didn't want to slam into their pointy sides.

✳

IN CAMP THAT night, alone in my tent, I pulled handfuls of clothing out of my stuff sack, looking for my second pair of socks. The bag was half the size of my torso—heavy like a body—and held all of my spare clothes for the summer. I spread them out on my sleeping bag and saw how they reflected my expectations. My notions about the weather were embedded in the thickness of my long underwear and the layers I chose. There was no cotton, no shorts or T-shirts.

Less than forty-eight hours before that moment, we had been spread out in an apartment in Yellowknife, making the choices we would carry for weeks into the unknown. Fleece clothing, toques, socks, bug shirts, books, and toiletries flooded the wall-to-wall carpet. We stood two by two with three empty packs. A tent, two sleeping bags, two Therm-a-Rests, and all of the clothes, books, and toiletries for two people had to fit into each pack. We had to be ruthless. And given the Tetris-like feat it would be to pack and close those packs every day, our pack partners would stay fixed throughout the trip.

Drew held up a pair of fleece pants. "Extras for the tent at night?" he said.

"Chuck 'em," Tim replied.

"If I only bring *War and Peace*, can I borrow a book from someone else?" asked Alie.

"I don't want to trade for *War and Peace*," said Drew, and we all laughed.

Jen sat with a collection of toques in her hands, mentally weighing their merits before choosing one in pale blue and a balaclava.

Levi laid out his clothes for the next day, and I agonized over my socks.

"Can I bring more than one pair of dry socks?" I asked.

"No!" came the chorus of replies.

I took out a collection of spiritual writings that I had inherited from Tim's mum, flipped to the end of the first section, and carefully split the book down the spine with my knife.

I made room for forty rolls of print and slide film (resisting the digital revolution), a point-and-shoot camera, and an old manual SLR camera with two lenses. I carried a personal journal and a group journal with recipes, our menu, and plenty of blank pages for the group log. I jammed pens and extra lighters into every bag and pocket. Tim had the smallest pile of personal gear, including a pair of binoculars that he would rarely remove from around his neck. Levi had two prized possessions: a handmade paddling shirt with blue pinstripes, and a barometer. He didn't keep a journal; he kept a weather log. Drew brought an old IBM baseball cap, courtesy of his dad, an executive at the company's Toronto office. He had sewed white cotton flaps around the hat's back rim to keep the bugs away from his neck and the sun off his freckles. Jen and Alie shared a passion for coffee, which they planned to make in Alie's insulated French press mug. They had begun coffee calculations months before and had already stashed several bundles of it throughout our food bags. Their coffee carried the spirit of Sunday morning: no day would start without it, no matter how much distance we needed to make. Alie left all other books behind so she could bring *War and Peace*. She had enviable bibbed rain pants and an ultra-wide-brimmed hat. Jen's big sunglasses looked great on her—even after they snapped in half and got repaired with duct tape—and they would protect her eyes from the north's signature days of long light and bright reflections. Her prized possession, however, turned out to be the balaclava. In Yellowknife it seemed like overkill, but on the river, it provided warmth and kept bugs away from her neck and ears.

When we had finally settled the bags and laid out paddling clothes for the morning, I grabbed the cordless phone and headed outside.

I stepped into the warmth of the evening sun in Yellowknife's Old Town, but the mosquitoes chased me back inside to cover up. I dragged my sleeping bag into the driveway and climbed under it to make my final calls.

First, I called Dad.

"Did you register with the RCMP?" he asked.

"Tomorrow."

"Got your first-aid kit?"

"Yep."

"Call me when you are out?"

"I promise, but promise me you won't worry unless we are overdue—and even then we are probably fine."

"Okay, dear."

"I love you, Dad."

"I love you, too. Have a good summer."

Next I called Mum and relayed the same information, a habit familiar to any child of divorced parents.

"I'm excited for you, Skunk," she said, invoking my pet name from childhood. "Be safe, eat lots, look after each other, and have fun."

"I will."

"Call me when you are out?"

"I promise, but promise me you won't worry unless we are overdue—and even then we are probably fine."

"I promise."

"I love you, Mum."

"I love you, too. Have a good summer."

I have made many of these calls over the years without thinking too much about what it might be like for my parents. It must be extra hard to say goodbye to an only child.

After hanging up, I stayed on a chair at the side of the driveway, sweating under the drape of my down-filled sleeping bag. From inside this sweltering cave, I made one more call. I hadn't planned on calling Dalton. We had said goodbye in Victoria, and I wasn't making any promises to him over the summer. I wanted to leave things open, to back away from the hint of commitment.

"Hey," I said. "I just thought I'd call to let you know we are leaving tomorrow."

"I'm so glad you called," he replied. He sounded tired.

I didn't have much to say. The mosquitoes had found my ankles, so I shared a few details about the bus ride and got ready to hang up.

"I love you, Jenny," he said.

"Okay. Thanks. Have a good summer."

THE CALLS AND packing choices were behind me now. I already knew I had made a mistake with that windbreaker. I pulled on soft, clean socks that cushioned my toes, and headed down to the kitchen. We always separated our sleeping and cooking areas to keep bears, who might be drawn to food smells, away from our tents.

"Come on!" called Jen. "We're going to test a banger."

Our bear-safety plan included a few pieces of equipment. First, an alarm made by stringing a trip wire around our well-sealed food cache and plugging it into a wallet-sized personal safety alarm; if the cache was disturbed, the wire would pull out of the alarm (we hoped), set it off, and alert us. Second, a plastic pistol that shot off bangers and screamers (like mini-flares) to keep bears back should they approach. Third, three cans of bear spray. We did not have a gun. It made perfect sense to test one or two of our fifty-odd bangers so that everyone would know how to use them. I couldn't explain the grip of anxiety I felt as Jen unpacked the bear bag and pulled out the Ziplocs full of red and green cartridges.

"We don't want to waste them," I said weakly.

"We need to know how they work," Jen replied.

"I just..." My voice trailed off as I imagined a bear zeroing in on our camp. Marking us. Circling for days, getting closer despite our repeated volleys of bangers and screamers. It would be my turn to hold the bear off, and I would reach into the plastic bag, powdery and acidic, only to find we had used every little packet of sound and light.

My irrational fear and mumblings of complaint continued as Jen jammed the cartridge in place and fired.

"There," she said. "Easy."

And she was on to the next thing, dinner, while I stood on the bank, trapped by my imagination.

✳

ON OUR SECOND night, rosy twilight seeped through the walls of the tent, enough light to see the map, even though it was nearly midnight. It was time to give the trip some structure: how would we reach our geographical target, 1,000 kilometers away, and what did we want to get out of the experience along the way?

I sat beside Tim, who spent most of the meeting staring at the floor. He'd had moments of levity during the day, but now he looked exhausted. I hoped he hadn't made a mistake by coming.

"We're living the dream now," Drew said.

"I think it would be good to go around and hear from everyone about their expectations for the trip," Alie said.

Choosing the Back River as our destination had taken weeks of debate on the phone, in emails, and in an online chat room, where we devoted hours to discussing the features we wanted from our route. We listed the pros and cons of various rivers, such as wildlife, beauty, topography, and length. We researched cost and travel logistics and got recommendations for dozens of routes. In the end, the Baillie and Back rivers showed up on everyone's lists.

"This is going to be a big challenge," Jen said, "but I'm trying not to have too many expectations. I mean, it's all so new. I don't really have specific goals."

I spoke up next. "I'd like to see some wildlife. I know we can't control that, but if we take time to stop and look, that will help a lot." I looked at Tim to see if he wanted to add anything, but he stayed quiet.

"As long as we keep moving," Levi said. He knew me well, and realized I would prefer time to explore on land over long days of paddling to keep on pace.

We chatted about the animals we wanted to see and what it was like for Drew and Jen to be on the tundra for the first time.

"I also wanted to talk about group dynamics," Alie said. "I think it's really important that we are open with each other and don't get into relationships that feel exclusive."

She looked over at Tim and me. "You guys are already really close—which is great. I just want to make sure everyone feels welcome around you."

I found this a strange thing to bring up so early. It's good to be proactive, but I didn't like being singled out for something I hadn't done yet. Alie was being sensitive, in a way. Just odd, given Tim's state. If he wanted to share some stuff privately with me, I hoped that wouldn't make us exclusive.

Silence fell. We waited for Tim, pretending that we weren't waiting.

"As you know," he started, "it's been two months since my mum died."

Tim's voice barely faltered. He talked about his mum: how much he loved her and how much they had been through; Tim's sister, Debbie, had died of cancer when she was twelve and Tim was nine.

After he finished, a high and hollow sound began outside. The six of us bent our heads, listening.

"Wolves," said Tim.

The volume of their keening rose until the calls of the pack were unmistakable. We exchanged looks and scrambled out of the tent. The tundra stretched around us, pink under the circling sun, but the wolves were nowhere to be seen. They quieted. Tim threw back his head and howled. Several moments passed, then the wolves called again, one voice and another and another until they crested a minor chord. They must have been just over the rise.

CHAPTER 2

FIRST MISTAKES

Wilderness has a pull on me, like a child yanking on my pant leg. I am always looking for fragments of the wild—combing the hedge for birds' nests, searching the boulevard for insects.

I was lucky to have parents who let me wander on my own to the pond near our Ontario cottage when I was young. I watched and then tried to catch anything that moved. I still remember the slippery push of a bullfrog's mouth forcing my fingers apart, a dragonfly hooked onto the thinness of my shoulder, a captured turtle in the washtub snipping at iceberg lettuce.

My early love of the outdoors stopped at canoeing, however. My father took me in his cedar-canvas canoe to paddle the streams and swamps of Algonquin Park, but that little boat bored me to distraction.

Canoeing was for adults. Supremely slow and quiet, a perfect place for that most hated adult activity—conversation. The monotony of canoeing only began to shift when I was allowed to take the canoe out alone, at age eight. Then I could spin my craft, fight its nose into the wind, and slip it out of sight into the trees. One day, I nudged the canoe up to a yellow lady's slipper, and as I pulled the flower down to my nose, a mother deer and her fawn stood up. I realized then that a canoe could help reveal the world's secrets; it could unlock the land.

I completed my first long canoe trip, with Tim, at the age of twenty-two. The two of us spent forty days exploring Northern Ontario's lakes and rivers until my paddle felt like an extension of my body. Throughout university, I would visit the map library and trace northern rivers with my fingers: scanning the topography of the North, examining landscapes stretched by the Mercator projection. At twenty-five, I went to the Arctic for the first time and paddled for fifty days on and around Nunavut's Hood River, that time with Tim, Levi, and three others. At twenty-eight, I was ready for the Back.

Leading up to the trip, I did my best to project confidence when talking to my parents and friends. Polar bears ripped me to pieces in my mind's eye, but I didn't let on.

＊

WE SHOVED AWAY from shore on the fourth afternoon, and I braced my knees wide against the hull, preparing to give Drew the power strokes he would need to steer us through the next set of rapids. It was Drew's first day in the stern. We'd already been through a few sets of swifts and small rapids that morning, but the next set would require more maneuvering.

We had all stopped to scout the rapids and don our helmets before committing ourselves to the river. We would do this with any stretch of moving water that wasn't completely straightforward.

The river was growing. The shore ice was melting; small streams and tributaries joined the Baillie's main flow. Waves and currents remained manageable, simple even, but we always had to be careful. The cold was our biggest threat.

We saw our next set from shore. An unobstructed chute led through a dark vee of smooth water. The vee piled into a row of standing waves, called haystacks, which are typical at the bottom of any rapid. They range from little bumps to powerful towers that swamp and flip canoes. These waves stood higher than any we had seen so far—big enough that we didn't want to hit them head on.

Drew and I planned to power through the current from river right to river left, taking advantage of the safe passage down the tongue but skirting the wave train at the bottom. By staying left of the big waves, we would avoid being swamped while remaining in the forward flow of the river and staying out of the confused water at the river's edge.

We waited until Tim and Alie hit the current.

"Are you ready?" I called over the rush.

"Yeah, let's go," Drew replied.

Drew sat straight-spined in the stern. A few wisps of orange hair stuck out from under his helmet. Wire-rimmed glasses, firmly tethered to a neck strap, sat on his freckled nose, and the high collar of a light gray turtleneck kept the wind and bugs out. His 5'10" frame filled the seat. He sported a bright yellow life vest, an orange whistle and matching helmet, and rubberized gloves. Thanks to the outfit, Jen had nicknamed him the Safety Officer.

I barely knew Drew before we met at the Edmonton bus station with all of our gear. He had been recommended by friends and had paddled with Levi on Ontario rivers; he seemed a good fit. From the beginning, he was keen to take on food preparation and to help with any aspect of the trip, though he was new to map research, northern logistics, and expedition equipment. He was easy to talk to and comfortable in a leadership role, though the Arctic would test him on that. Drew laughed easily and made lots of jokes. He was quick to pose for silly pictures and eager to learn. I thought we would be well suited as paddling partners.

We pushed off.

My paddle bit the water as I strained to pull us forward faster than the river. To maintain our ability to steer, we needed to accelerate beyond the speed of the current. Drew pointed our boat left of the waves as we accelerated downstream. The river wanted to wash us into the haystacks, and Drew struggled to keep us moving across the current. It is the same race every time, every rapid. The river wants one thing, and we want something else.

I pulled hard to give us speed, but the tongue held us in its gravity. It swiveled our nose toward the waves. I bent my upper body out over the river and heaved on my paddle, trying to correct the angle. Drew pulled and pulled, but our bow was already at the foot of the first wave, which sucked us down and then threw us up in a crash of spray, shooting me skyward. The next rise sent me through a window of water, as polished as plate glass, that pooled around my knees. Our target swished by my left side as we bucked into the next wave—another lapful of water. Then I felt

Drew pulling us left, heading for shore, turning us broadside. I sensed his terror, quickly followed by my own.

"No, no!" I screamed. "Forward, straight into it, forward!"

I swung my paddle to the starboard side and pulled us back into the waves. Now that we were in them, we had to ride them out. Straight ahead, full of water, became the safest exit. We rose up again and dropped back to the river. The waves mellowed—our boat teetered to the bank and stopped.

I didn't know what to say. It was a mistake to miss our line and hit the waves, but that seemed like a simple miscalculation with the drawback of getting soaked. What worried me was Drew's compensation. Riding big waves is one thing; trying to pull out of them is another. Our safest play was through the stacks. Did he know that? I didn't want to challenge him, but I worried about the bigger water coming up.

I looked back at my partner and tried to laugh it off with a joke: "Pass me a towel and some shampoo?"

THE NEXT DAY, it was my turn.

I sat on a stone near our camp stove and sipped my tea—black chai with milk powder and honey. I watched the Baillie glide by and thought ahead to the day. The haystack incident had shaken me. Drew and I had talked about it, but not very well.

"That was kind of crazy."

"Cold water."

"Yeah."

"More practice I guess, eh?"

The fact remained that I had overridden Drew's call when I pulled us back into the waves. We hadn't been on the same page. I felt the onus was on me to keep us safe.

A bright sky helped lift my nervousness. My sense of warm and cold was beginning to recalibrate, and the breeze felt balmy. It would speed the disappearance of the remaining ice. Warm. Still no bugs.

Drew and I climbed into our boat and onto a long series of moderate rapids. We bounced downstream and negotiated vees and small channels. The river grew every moment.

Pools of water with upstream flow, called eddies, form behind obstructions in the river, such as rocks or sandbars. When the current is strong enough, it creates lines of turbulence that separate the downstream current from the eddy. Those eddy lines were different by that fifth day; they swirled and bubbled with force. The river had crossed a threshold overnight.

We pulled over after lunch to scout another rapid. Drew and I picked our way across the bouldery shore to stand by the main funnel.

"What do you think?" Drew asked.

"If we come across the vee from left to right we can punch through that eddy line and take a rest down there," I said, pointing to a pool of calm water. "Hey, Tim, Levi? Are you guys heading for that eddy?"

"That's what I was thinking," said Tim.

Levi nodded.

We would proceed in our regular order: Tim and Alie in front, Drew and me in the middle, Levi and Jen at the back.

Tim and Alie looked at us from their boat and touched their helmets, signaling "Okay." We signaled back; they pushed away from shore and disappeared around the bend.

"Straight through the vee and eddy out on river right," I said to Drew. "Ready?"

"Ready."

We made our signal, and I pushed us away from the bank. Drew pulled us to midstream; I pried with my paddle to set our angle and aim for the vee. We pulled hard to gain speed, and black water passed beneath us. Noise rushed up from curling waves downstream, and shallow rocks threw sound and spray toward us. The vee itself was silent.

The current smoothed after we passed the rapid's throat, and I looked to the eddy line. Maintain speed, set the angle, lean into it. Our bow hit the line, and Drew lifted his arms to plant his paddle in the opposing flow of the eddy; I swept from the back, and the world slowed. Our boat sat too upright, and my angle was wrong. We glanced off the line. We couldn't pierce it.

The river didn't hesitate.

It grabbed our downstream gunwale amidships and pulled down hard. I watched the side go under; I threw my weight to the right. *Can I stop it?* The boat keeled back toward center, then plunged under again. My ankles strained against my running shoes as the water hit my left arm, then my hip. *Get your feet out.* I leaned across the right gunwale, trying to keep my head dry. Our green hull flipped up beside me; I could touch it. My legs were still twisted under the stern seat—I yanked them hard into the water.

I fought fear to fill my lungs. *It's not that cold.* I floated in the cocoon of my heat. *Swim.* Damp warmth stayed close to my skin until the river found my neck; then it rushed everywhere at once. Down my chest, my legs; up my sleeves, my belly. It burned like heat at first. Heat is what it wanted.

My head went under. The boat pulled away with the river.

I fought back to the surface and Drew appeared beside me.

"Swim!" I yelled.

We both set our angle toward shore, using the current to help us cross the eddy line—I was amazed that I remembered to do this—but the eddy wouldn't yield. We were close to shore, but we couldn't punch through the line. Ten strokes. My body gave its heat to the river so quickly. I flipped on my back. My arms barely cleared the water.

"Grab on, grab the stern!" I heard Tim and Alie screaming. They had paddled back to the eddy line to rescue us.

"Jenny, grab on!"

I wondered how long they had been there before I heard them.

I swung my arms, heavy with the river, up onto the stern deck, then floated my legs up. Drew did the same at the bow. Arms and legs out of the water, I won back some time. Tim and Alie paddled for shore, fighting the turbulence to get away, hindered by our drag on their boat. I pulled myself together: "You're okay; you can do it," I repeated aloud until the bow made shore and Tim reached down to drag me up the rocks.

Drew took off like a shot, running down the beach.

"What happened?" he said, over and over. He was furious.

I stumbled across the river-washed stones and started pulling my clothes off. Drew ran back and forth trying to get warm, then veered away from the river toward a cluster of muskox.

I yelled after him, my first words since the river, "Look out for the muskox! They charge, you know!"

My white skin reflected the sun as I stood naked on the shore. I felt like a skeleton. The water had flowed right through me, and now the wind.

I shook uncontrollably while Alie and Tim pulled spare clothes over my wet legs and across my back. I focused on getting dressed and watching the rocks at my feet. Alie pulled a down coat around me, and I crumpled onto a rock. She circled behind and wrapped me in her arms and legs until I stilled.

Jen ran up with some dried fruit and a thermos of tea. They had seen our dump and rushed their boat downstream to rescue ours.

"We got the boat and chased down one loose barrel. We only lost one paddle." We had extras.

Tim went to check on Drew, who was still pacing the beach, refusing to change his clothes.

"I'm not cold," he said, pale with shock.

TIM, JEN, LEVI, and Alie laid our clothes out on the rocks to dry. Thank God for the sun. We pitched our tents 100 meters away on the flat tundra and cooked by the river, but not too close. Everyone worked on supper except me. I sat dazed by the overturned canoe. *What will happen now?* The Baillie stays swift over long sections. We were lucky to be near the eddy. I could barely swim after one minute, so I would never have made it to shore from mid-channel.

Drew had suffered some shock, but his size and weight, combined with our short exposure, guarded him from hypothermia. I was 6 feet tall and weighed only 140 pounds, so mild hypothermia grabbed me easily. It had felt close to something more serious. Aside from the dangers, I brooded over my sense of failure. Everyone else had hit the line.

Drew walked toward me.

"I'm sorry," he said.

"It was my fault," I replied. "Not enough angle."

"I got really angry afterwards, but not at you. I wanted to make sure you knew that."

We reviewed our mistakes: we hadn't anticipated the change in current; we weren't going fast enough. Underneath that, another truth: I was rusty, Drew inexperienced. The river would only get bigger from here.

We gathered by the stove for tundra pizza, a thick bannock crust spread with rehydrated tomato sauce, onions, red and green peppers, pineapple, and cheese (gluey, vegan "cheese" for Levi).

After dinner, Tim came and sat beside me. "Stop worrying. You can do this."

We drew diagrams of the river in my journal and reviewed the basics of eddy turns: Power. Angle. Tilt.

✳

AFTER A COLD and rainy breakfast the next day, we convened in our wet suits, looking like neoprene ninjas. An entire day in a rubber suit is dank and itchy, but nobody complained. The suits would increase our safety margin and help us regain confidence.

Levi and Tim took turns reviewing river rescue, and we congratulated each other on what we'd pulled off the preceding afternoon. Drew and I had remembered our swift-water swimming technique, the lead boat had fetched us, and the sweep boat had gone after the gear. We had treated shock and mild hypothermia effectively. But we had still dumped, and I didn't want to think about the consequences if the lead boat had gone down with no one in the eddy to help.

Next, we triple-checked the emergency communications gear we had stowed in accessible places only four days before. Our satellite phone lay cushioned in dark gray foam, inside a durable, waterproof case at the top of a pack. It looked like an oversized cordless phone, with the buttons protected by a plastic guard that flipped down. The antenna was as long as the phone and as thick as three pencils, and it folded out to point at the sky and improve reception. Although we could use the phone anytime to call home, we had agreed not to. We wanted to maintain a sense of isolation and separation from the rest of the world, plus we wanted to conserve the batteries in case of an emergency. The only phone we could get in Yellowknife was a Globalstar brand, which was not as reliable north of sixty—but we weren't going to the North Pole, and if it was the northern rental phone of choice, we figured it would work fine.

The phone would handle emergency communication, and for emergency evacuation we packed a small satellite signal called a Personal Locator Beacon, or PLB. A $900 waterproof gadget (which is less expensive these days), the PLB was slightly larger than our phone and covered in hard plastic. It had been adapted from airplane and shipping technology for the wilderness recreation market. No signal would be sent unless we followed the simple instructions stenciled on the side of its yellow plastic shell: *Remove cover. Push button.* That one button would summon the closest search-and-rescue crews. Stern advisories on the registration papers warned that it was exclusively for life-threatening situations. "So not if you have a fight with your boyfriend?" my mum had joked before we left.

There is no perfect location for any of these things; you just have to maximize your chances of being close enough to one or the other device in an emergency. We decided to keep the phone with our gear and to strap the PLB around somebody's waist. Levi's level head and experience, plus his meticulous care of our gear and equipment, won him the honor of wearing our life-saving fanny pack.

The last point of business was paddling partners. It made sense for Drew and me to split up for a while and for him to paddle with Levi, the person he trusted most. That put Jen with me, the stern person who had botched a simple eddy turn the day before.

She was visibly nervous but flashed me a big smile. "We can do it," she said.

Jen was our most novice paddler. I had often sterned, but only with another practiced paddler in my bow. It was time to step up, even though I wanted to hide under a rock. I tried to exude confidence.

On the water, Jen eased my worry almost immediately. She was confident and trusting. With each draw stroke (a lateral pull that turns the bow quickly), Jen reached out and pulled hard. When we needed to lean, she leaned. When I asked her to paddle forward, she didn't worry about the rocks ahead. She brought the same attitude to the boat as she did to the trip: Don't overthink; just do it.

Drew was still badly shaken. He was happy to be paddling with Levi, but he looked pale. He missed his wife. And his wooden torso would not lean away from the boat's midline—a critical skill for a bow paddler.

"I feel totally responsible for him," Levi told me later. "He's here because of me."

CHAPTER 3

WILDING

We saw our first lone caribou on Day 6. It stood in water up to its ankles near shore. Its legs must have burned in the cold river. We had caught the caribou midcrossing, but it wouldn't go back the way it came; two white wolves waited on the bank. The first sat back on its haunches halfway up the hill, while the other crouched at the top, outlined by the sky. All three animals stared at us. Nobody moved. Had we saved the caribou's life, at least for the moment? We silently agreed to climb the bank on our side of the river, lie down on our bellies, and watch. The first wolf placed its head on its paws and stared at us. We stood out like Gore-Tex flags.

Ten minutes had passed when Levi looked over his shoulder.

"There's a grizzly bear back there," he said calmly.

"Let's go back to the boats," said Jen. "Right?"

The grizzly moved slowly between low bushes, 200 meters distant, pausing now and then to sniff. The wind kept our scent away.

"It's not paying any attention to us," said Tim.

Jen and Drew exchanged looks but didn't move, and we stayed bracketed, like the caribou, between two wolves and a grizzly. I nested my elbows between the crowberry bushes and let my chin rest in my hands. I breathed in the cold aroma of the tundra.

*

WE HAD BEEN surrounded by wildlife from the moment we arrived on the Baillie River, but it took some time for that to sink in. Despite total immersion, it was scenery at first, like a movie, only colder. Going into the wild is like going to sleep; you get there in stages.

The immersion in ice water helped me sink myself into everything else. By the end of that first week, as the rest of my life fell away, scenes from our first few days asserted themselves in my memory. There had been pintails and red-throated loons the day we landed. Then Arctic terns, as light as tissue paper mobiles, dive-bombed us midriver. Those tiny ambassadors called to mind the other birds, including snow geese, eiders, plovers, sandpipers, gulls, and jaegers, who stream north every year to find country lush enough to feed and fledge their young. On the second day, we had seen muskox at lunch. The soft underfur that protects them all winter was beginning to loosen, and it hung from their backs like dreadlocks. After that, more wolves, a lake trout following my lure, more muskox, and a woolly bear caterpillar—amber and black and slow. Partway through a drawling sunset, while we set up the kitchen for supper, an Arctic fox took on two Canada geese, trying to steal eggs from their nest. The fox had already traded its white winter fur for the brown-with-a-white-tummy summer version—Arctic foxes are the only canids in the world that change color with the seasons. This fox would have been on the move during winter and may even have visited another continent—Arctic foxes sometimes travel 2,000 kilometers across land and sea ice in a single year. By spring, they are more likely to stay put and take advantage of super-abundant food sources. They'll eat seaweed, mollusks, garbage, and insects if they have to, but they prefer lemmings and voles when they are plentiful. Eggs are another favorite. Foxes cruise the margins of breeding bird colonies or stake out individual nests, as we saw. In some places, the little thieves take an annual average of over a thousand eggs *each*. The match we witnessed between the geese and the fox was surprisingly even. The geese reared up on their legs and spread their wings wide. They stretched their necks, opened their mouths, and hissed and screamed while beating their wings in the fox's face. The fox found itself boxed out repeatedly but kept bobbing and weaving like a featherweight. Fake left, stab right. Dart, spin, spring in for the egg.

During that first week, sporadic visits from mosquitoes and blackflies reminded us to tuck our pants into our socks and to keep our cuffs tight and our necks covered. It was still too cold for the legendary swarms that would crowd our wrists and eyes. Once the weather warmed, they would bite anything they could reach. Blackflies specialize in getting into your clothes; mosquitoes focus on what's exposed. Almost every historical account of summer travel in the tundra by non-indigenous people has at least one sickening tale of the swarms that leave you bleeding or weeping or both. Last time I had been north, my neck was so swollen from the bites that I couldn't look up at the sky. One day, I blew my nose and seven blackflies came out. Every cold day spared us from the torture we knew was coming.

✳

I MAINTAINED A list of wildlife sightings, along with a bug index, in my journal. I wrote in it every evening. We also kept a group journal, and everyone took turns recording our collective experience—so some nights I wrote two versions of the same day.

I started keeping a journal when I was nine years old. The summer after my dad moved out, Mum decided that we would go on a road trip, and she bought me two diaries to take along—one large and one small, both covered in white fabric printed with wavy orange and blue vertical lines. I loved that they felt like clothing.

We piled our suitcase, bathing suits, and books into the back of our gray Oldsmobile Firenza and left Ottawa in search of La Gaspésie, the peninsula in Quebec that reaches for the Atlantic from the south shore of the St. Lawrence. It must have been one hell of a trip for my mother. It was her first holiday as a single parent while my dad was still settling in with the woman he had left her for. Maybe Mum was anxious—worried about money, scared about the future—but I don't remember any of that, though I do recall writing down our expenses in the smaller of my two books. We stayed in small whitewashed motels by the sea that cost $25 a night. We stood on seaside cliffs and ate in family restaurants. Mum bought me a men's XXL T-shirt that said "Gaspé" in black cursive, and I wore it everywhere with my bathing suit underneath. Every night Mum and I would sit on our beds, cross-legged, and write in our diaries.

That journey was hardly a wilderness trip, but my strongest memories are from the wildest places we visited. We hiked out to Percé Rock and almost got trapped by the rising tide. I felt the water drag at my ankles, and its power frightened me. We visited gannet colonies where thousands of birds with plumage like molded plastic stared the ocean down. We saw fishing boats and fishermen ready to take on the waves. I learned, from watching my mother, that visiting wild, foreign places—even if they aren't that far from home—is like pushing the pause button. And when the shit hits the fan, the wilder the better.

The year I turned eleven, my mum took another big trip, this time to the Nahanni River in the Northwest Territories, and this time on her own.

My dad had been gone two years by then, and Mum had cancer again, though we didn't know it yet. At least I didn't. She had a funny lump in her groin, and sometimes she would let me push it in with my finger and watch it bounce back. It was hard and springy, about the size of a golf ball. She said it didn't hurt.

Mum booked a two-week guided canoe trip on the Nahanni for that summer. She would get the thing looked at afterwards. It wouldn't be good, so she might as well ride a wild river before solving the mystery. She had already survived a melanoma; she was forty-one years old.

Before Mum left, a friend gave her some good advice: "Bring lots of cigarettes." The logic was that everyone else would use the trip to try to quit, but they would soon be bumming, so if she planned to smoke, she should bring extras. The lump would force her to quit soon enough.

In the pictures, my mother looks remarkably like me: tall, thin, a bit slouchy, and wide-smiling. She also had a mop of curls, though hers was a perm.

When she got home, Mum gushed about the trip; she couldn't stop. I didn't mind hearing the stories at first, but soon other things took over. The lump turned out to be a malignant tumor. There was surgery, hospital time, and a gruesome, foot-long scar. Every day, nurses arrived at our house and dragged sopping yellow gauze out of a hole in my mum's leg while I watched.

As the scar healed and Mum successfully fought her nicotine cravings, she would go on and on about the trip. The big barrel and the ex-marine who liked to carry it. The neurotic couple in matching Gore-Tex. The handsome guide who cooked her supper. The guy with Crohn's who insisted on his own tent. I rolled my eyes every time she brought it up. The stories were endless and repetitive and—God, Mum, enough! You told me that already.

I didn't realize until years later, in a forehead-slapping moment, that this was her this-could-be-my-last-trip trip. There's-a-goddamned-lump-in-my-leg-and-I-might-not-paddle-again trip.

After I successfully nagged her into shutting up about it, I wanted the stories back. "What was that guy's name again?" "How did you dump your boat?"

TOWARD THE END of the first week, we gathered in our biggest tent, a four-season dome that we had started calling

The Boss (everything gets named on a canoe trip), for another talk. We were still new to that landscape—and always would be—but even as we figured out our gear, our food, and our paddling partners, we needed to think about the ending. We had 1,080 kilometers to travel and fifty days in which to do it. A few too many slow days, combined with the weather wild card, and that goal could quickly become impossible. We spent the first few minutes smearing bugs against the ceiling while Levi laid out the maps. He tugged some from our small, semi-sodden map case, which looked like a glorified Ziploc bag but was never dry, and pulled another stack from the map tube, a simple, waterproof poster tube that held oracle-like status. It told us the future, and we needed it. Stuffed with 1:250,000-scale maps for the big picture and dozens of 1:50,000s for a closer look, the map tube was carefully strapped into the bow of the same boat every day. Each map had been photocopied to save money. Backup 1:250s lived in a second boat.

The maps crinkled as we spread them out and shoved them under our knees. As we ran our fingers over the land, we scanned for white-water symbols and eyeballed the big lakes coming up.

"We are here," said Levi, placing his finger on a large-scale map. "We have fifty days to get here." His finger skated across one map, onto the next, and up to an island on the Arctic coast. "We need some milestones."

Levi's calm, logical demeanor was a tremendous asset to our group. He was very open-minded, and somewhat absent-minded, but also fastidious about repairs, safety, and scouting. He told obscure jokes, had no appreciation for sarcasm, and made us laugh with his dance performances and funny songs. His whole look—trim frame, steady brown eyes, dark hair and matching beard—inspired trust.

Levi had grown up in British Columbia in a six-sided log house that his parents had built. They had been career tree planters who lived off the grid and home-schooled their kids. It worked fine until Levi went on strike in grade three; he refused to do any more work until they moved to town and put him in a real school. By the time I met him in 2002, he had both a bachelor's and a master's in physics and was working on his PhD. A few years after the Back River trip, he would be a post-doctoral fellow in biostatistics at Harvard University's prestigious cancer research institute, working in a challenging new field he hadn't formally studied. He was that smart, as well as quirky. We had become good friends on our first Arctic trip three years before, and I was thankful to travel with him again. There was no doubt that he would get along with everyone.

That night, he held down the maps and reviewed our plan. We had planned on 30 kilometers a day plus seven rest days and seven weather days, give or take. That gave us a total of fifty days, and we booked our flights out of Gjoa Haven, on King William Island, another five days after that, to be safe. My eyes moved back and forth over the maps. Even though I had studied them a hundred times back home, it all looked different now that the real landscape pressed against the door.

"What about the lakes?" I asked. The Back is famous for the Garry Lakes, a string of huge, shallow bodies of water that stretch for hundreds of kilometers. They were about a week away.

"We might have to paddle nights," said Alie. "We did that on one of my other trips. It helped us keep the distance up when the weather got shitty." The lakes were the biggest threat to our timeline. You could sit a long, long time waiting for the wind to die.

We chipped away at a plan for the next hour or so. With string and an old map roller to measure distance, we went over the route in detail:

— 206 kilometers to the confluence with the Back;
— 420 to the start of Pelly Lake, the beginning of the flat-water stretch;
— 610 to Rock Rapids, the most turbulent part of the river;
— 930 to the Hayes River junction, at the cusp of the river's mouth and its delta;
— 150 kilometers of ocean paddling to reach Montreal Island, our final pickup point;
— Total distance remaining: 1080 kilometers.

"There will be lots to explore along the way," I said. "It would be nice to take some rest days because we want to, not just when we have to."

"We need time to stop for wildlife too," said Tim. "That's one of the reasons we came up here."

"I agree that's important, but obviously we need to get to the end in time. If we take too much time early on, it worries me a little," said Alie.

"We've set a big objective. We can't get away from that," said Jen.

"I'm excited about all of it," said Drew, "but I want to meet the goal."

"We all want to meet the goal," I replied.

"Rapids take time too," said Levi. "It will be hard to make 30 kilometers when there's lots of white water."

"And easy with a good current or a tailwind," said Tim.

These are the struggles of every group trip—who is there to paddle hard and meet the goal, who is there to explore the landscape and take their time. Each one of us was a mix of both, to varying degrees. We had all committed to the same objective, but there would be more than one way to reach it.

That night, the tiny crack that had opened between us was barely noticeable, and we were very polite about it. Some pushed to get the distance under our belt and rest later, if we had time; some, mainly Tim and I, pushed for a slower pace to enjoy experiences as they came and deal with weather challenges if we had to. Pace is critical on a long trip, and finding a balance between enjoyment and achievement can be tricky.

"Look," Jen said finally, "we've already cut the trip up into chunks."

"So we can do one chunk at a time," Drew finished.

We could have rest time and fun time, as long as we made the end of the section by the agreed-upon day. It was the logical compromise. Depending on what lay ahead—what rapids, what weather—we might have to scrap the plan and make a new one anyway.

My biggest hope, and the reason I wanted extra time at the beginning of the trip, was for the caribou. I wanted to see a herd. In early spring, barren-ground caribou calve in the northern tundra—beyond the range of wolves, their biggest predators, who stay further south to den. After calving, the male, female, and young caribou aggregate in the tens of thousands for a long journey south to the tree line. They spend the midsummer walking skinny trails that have been pounded into the muskeg by previous generations. They graze and rest in between hours of travel, when they move in lines or loose groups. The trails lead them back to the subarctic forest, the northern limits of the taiga, where they will rut and mate and spread out to forage over the winter. The distance between their calving and wintering grounds can be as much as 1,000 kilometers. I had always hoped to meet them somewhere along the way.

During my first forty-six days on the tundra in 2002, we paddled the Hood River and sections of the Coppermine, farther to the west, and we saw one caribou. One. A single representative of a species that is hundreds of thousands strong. But you have to be in the right place at the right time to see them. We weren't.

On the Back, I had another chance. I imagined it over and over. The way they might appear over a rise and fill the valley like floodwater breaking away from a riverbed. The maps, books, and websites had told us we were most likely to cross paths with the caribou during the first half of our trip. So the caribou were another reason to take our time early on. But caribou are smoke in the wind, hard to find and impossible to plan for. So maybe it would be better to carry on in case of big storms.

Whatever our pace, I resolved to search for those caribou. The day after our planning session, and on many days thereafter, I climbed a ridge to examine the view rock by rock, inch by inch. I searched up every tributary valley that we passed. I never returned to the tent after a midnight pee without making a 360-degree scan. I wanted the experience for myself, but also for Tim, who loves wilderness more than anyone I know. It would be a salve for his grief.

✳

BY CANADA DAY, Day 7, the temperature had dropped below zero with a serious windchill. We were breaking in our new paddling teams and forming our six-person mini-culture by naming everything we had. Jen and I paddled her red boat, officially christened *Delilah*; Alie and Tim cruised in the blue 18-footer, *Bluebell*; Drew and Levi piloted the green 17-foot boat we called *The Frou-Frou Barge* in honor of Drew's stick collection lashed to the deck amidships. It's tough to have campfires in a land without trees, but if you are a diligent collector, like Drew, you can eke out the occasional cooking fire from willow branches and the odd piece of driftwood.

At lunchtime we jumped out of the boats where the shelter of the leeward bank let the brush grow thigh high, which meant it towered over everything else. We were so hungry we had to stop, so cold we had to keep moving. I ran back and forth, jumped, jumping-jacked, and jogged. Tim searched for the blessed thermoses of tea and couldn't find them. This was the worst news yet. I seriously considered a 15-kilometer tundra bushwhack back to the previous campsite.

"I could be there in, like, an hour. Or two."

As the threat of cold soup for the rest of the summer began to sink in, Tim—upside down under the spray deck—emerged with a flourish.

"Got 'em."

Back on the water, we came upon several small groups of Canada geese, a frequent sight along the banks. Jen and Drew found this a little bit too much Toronto, but I loved to see these birds in their wild, migratory incarnation. At that time each year, the geese drop their flight feathers, grounding them for a few weeks while they grow new ones. The birds stick close to the water while they wait. If a predator approaches over land, a quick dash to the river is their only escape. Because we came toward them from the water, they would sprint away over land in a rustle of feathers. They looked like Victorian ladies with their skirts pulled up around their knees.

Later that afternoon, our second bear of the trip sauntered over the hill and saw us paddling below, not 100 meters away. He didn't slow down to check us out but continued along the ridge with his cowboy swagger—hips swinging side to side. Like he was strolling the strip, looking for babes. A moment later, his eyes locked onto a solitary goose, a second before it saw him. The goose raced toward the river at full speed, but the bear was much faster. One moment he had been strolling; the next, ready to kill. The bear swooped over the goose, catching it above the shoulder in one smooth motion and then loping back to the top of the ridge. He snapped that goose left and right until it hung like a skein of wool.

The geese weren't fast enough for the wolves either. We happened upon a wolf biting through one—feathers stuck to fur—and then chasing down another. A second wolf crouched in the background with a radio collar hanging darkly from its neck.

Ever since the second night, when Tim had spoken of his mum and the wolves sang, each sighting made me think of Kathy. Their chorus sounded like a memory but more real. Wolves appeared to us as Kathy had become: more than shadow, less than flesh.

✳

THE MORNING AFTER we'd made our plan, my fingers burned with cold as I stuffed handfuls of wet nylon into the tent bag. Tim stood behind me, gazing across the tundra. I was about to kick his boot to wake him up but instead I followed his gaze. Two more wolves, or maybe some we had already seen, watched our every move.

After bulgur and cheese hash for breakfast, and with a clear goal in mind, we set out on our most ambitious day so far: 46 kilometers to the confluence with the Back River. We were tired from the first week of a life we weren't used to, and if we reached our goal, we could take a day off. When our energy flagged, Drew pulled out his special fuel: a super-deluxe multilayered snack of sour keys, tofu jerky, sundried tomatoes, and dried apples with cinnamon.

Life on the Baillie had been a kind of tug-of-war for me. The excitement of beginning the journey and seeing so many animals vied with frustration at feeling so cold and worry about getting along as a group: I wasn't laughing at the jokes; I felt like an outsider. I hoped that arriving at the Back would help smooth it all out.

The river was generous to us that day.

Jen turned to me: "It's like a conveyor belt."

Stroke by stroke we moved toward the river that would be our home for the rest of the summer. Tim was silent in the stern of his boat. I kept looking ahead, waiting for the sandy gates of the Back to show themselves.

CHAPTER 4

SINKING

Six giant bowls of pasta steamed on the edge of our kitchen rock. I wondered if Levi and Drew had doubled the recipe by accident. With this meal, we would celebrate our arrival at the confluence of the Baillie and the Back.

"I'll go get Tim," I said, and walked toward the tents. "Supper!" I called, but he didn't answer.

I scanned the tundra for him, then dropped to my knees and pulled the zipper to his tent.

"Tim?"

He lay on his right side with his chest to the wall. I dove in and closed the mesh to keep out the bugs.

"Tim?" I repeated softly, but he didn't move. He was sobbing into his sleeping bag, dragging uneven breaths into his lungs. I sat for a while and listened; my mind wandered back to Ontario and the days we had spent together before Kathy's funeral. He had cried a lot, but I'd never seen him like this.

"Oh dear," I said quietly, sounding like my grandma.

I lay down behind my friend and put an arm over his, each of his breaths now jolting both of us. Gray fog seeped from Tim's chest into mine. *Does he even know I'm here?*

Eventually, his breath slowed. I hoped he would be taken by a good dream. I sat up and looked at his face. It looked old. His body sank into the tundra, like a river cutting its own banks. I tumbled back outside and returned to my cold supper.

"Tim isn't having dinner tonight," I said through my tears. "He's sleeping."

※

BEFORE THE TRIP, I hadn't thought much about the effect Tim's grief might have on the rest of us, but I feared that he would stay behind. I wanted to travel with my friend, and the tundra was the best place I could imagine to receive the stream of his sadness. It wouldn't ricochet off the walls of the city or reflect back to him from the faces of others. Grief could pour out and sink into the moisture of the land. Be absorbed into the frozen soil. Disappear.

Tim and I met in our first-year botany lab at the University of Guelph. He had recently quit traveling North America and Europe as a downhill ski racer after a crash that broke his shoulder, both arms, and several fingers. I was fresh out of high school in Ottawa. The first time we hung out, we visited our professor and his electron microscope. We loved the same things: birds, canoes, and cruising campus with me on the handlebars of Tim's gold-painted bicycle.

We knew each other for two years before we crossed the boundary between friendship and courtship. On our first date, in October, he took me fly-fishing. He lent me his waders and spent the afternoon up to his waist in the river wearing shorts and gumboots.

Once we started dating, Tim and I planned our first long canoe trip in Northern Ontario. We shared the dream of being in the woods long enough for a different rhythm to emerge—a rhythm of camping and paddling. Maybe then we would feel what it was like to live outside, instead of visiting.

We didn't have any experience with long trips. Neither of us had been to summer camp, the usual Canadian training ground for such things, so we found an online trip report from a boy's summer camp and resolved to follow it for forty days through northwestern Ontario. We would start 500 kilometers north of Thunder Bay and hop between lakes and rivers neither of us had ever heard of, such as Bamaji, Zionz, Otoskwin, Attawapiskat, Kagianagami, and Ogoki.

We tree-planted to raise money for our trip, then came home to measure flour, rice, salt, and oats into bags. We bought a boat and convinced my mum to drive us three long days to the start point. The remoteness of the trip sank in when Dr. Rick, Tim's dad, walked us through the deluxe first-aid kit he had put together. The waterproof bag contained large dressings, splints, several varieties of antibiotics, a suture kit, and syringes for administering Demerol. I freaked when I saw the hypodermic needles.

"I don't know how to give an injection!"

"If things get that bad," Rick replied, "a needle will be the least of your worries. Just stick it in the thigh somewhere."

During the first week of the trip, my hands swelled and then toughened like dry paper. My shoulders, wrists, ankles, and back tightened and strained, then relaxed into the pull of my paddle. Heavy loads got lighter as we penetrated farther into the maze of conifer-dappled sunlight, afternoon thunderstorms, and the lichen's dry heat. Our route plan kept us paddling and portaging for most of the daylight hours, and we were still falling behind. Our metabolisms soared. It didn't take us long to realize that we hadn't brought enough food.

It rained for twenty-five days out of forty on that trip. I got beaver fever, our camera broke, Tim's foot got infected after he stepped in a nest of leeches, and we were hungry every day. It was the best summer ever.

We looked forward to the year ahead. Back in civilization, however, we lost our stride. We started getting on each other's nerves and couldn't agree on the simplest things. It wasn't the wilderness that broke us, as many people had predicted; it was coming home. We promised to stay friends, and, by a combination of love and stubbornness, we did. I wouldn't give up on my friend who could find joy while huddled under a tarp in a thunderstorm, eating cold barley stew from a Ziploc bag.

Three summers after Ontario, we planned our first canoe trip in the Arctic, and three years after that we set our sights on the Back. In between, we moved between the Rockies and the coast, working on conservation projects or taking jobs as wildlife guides, and we often ended up in the same town. By the time we hit the Back River, we had spent over 150 days camping together.

Tim turned thirty in 2005. A few wrinkles around his bright blue eyes creased his freckled face, and his short brown hair was getting sparse. Surgery after a ski accident left him with a plate in his arm and a scar like model train tracks to show for it. It pained him when he paddled or carried a canoe, but he rarely let on.

✺

ON APRIL 24, 2005, Tim's dad, Rick, and his mum, Kathy, drove from Barrie to London, Ontario, to visit family. Tim and I lived in Victoria, British Columbia, at the time. Out of the blue, Kathy suffered a second massive heart attack, eight years after her first. Kathy was alive but in a coma, and she wasn't expected to survive. By the time I got the news a few hours later, Tim had already left for the east.

The prognosis was not good but not certain, and Kathy had beaten the odds once already, making a remarkable recovery from her first heart attack. Kathy was a true believer in the power of positive thinking, and Tim spent four days by his mother's side in intensive care practicing everything he had learned from her. He held her hand, told stories, played guitar, and sang. He forbade the doctors or nurses to say anything negative within his mum's earshot. Kathy lay still.

On the evening of April 27, Tim called my house in Victoria from the hospital. "We're taking my mum off life support tonight." His voice was quiet. "We don't know how long she will last."

I bought a ticket over the counter and boarded a plane at 11:00 p.m. As I hurtled through the air from the Pacific coast, my eyes dry and unwilling to close, Tim sat alone with his mum—her eyes opening only at the sound of his voice.

When I landed in Toronto and called the hospital in London, Kathy's intensive-care nurse told me that Kathy was still alive. I sped down Highway 401 while Tim sat alone in his mum's hospital room and held her hand. She took a lungful of air, one deep breath, and died.

I burst into the hospital's sterile brightness two hours later. Tim walked alone in a blaze of white linoleum; he had just left her room after saying goodbye. He looked up in the final steps, reached his arms around my neck, and breathed, "My mummy's gone. My mummy's gone." I held tightly to his shoulders and cried silently, my mouth open against his shirt.

By afternoon on the same day, Tim and his dad were ready to go home to Barrie. Tim asked if I would come and stay with them. Rick hadn't been home since he and Kathy had left on vacation the week before. At the house, the evening air was thick with the smell of annuals and mown grass. The keys jingled on their way to the lock, and as Rick pushed the door open he instinctively blocked it with his shin to keep the cats from escaping. The unique Kathy-and-Rick's-house smell poured out. I wondered if the smell would change.

With Rick's permission, I cleaned out the leftovers from the fridge—Kathy's cooking packaged in Tupperware. The space that she had occupied surrounded me as I fussed in her kitchen. I kept myself busy: cleaning dishes, doing laundry, wiping dust. I walked to the basement laundry room and folded Kathy's small T-shirts that hung from the rack.

Three days later, Tim and I drove to the funeral service together in Kathy's car. It was a sunny spring day, and a small crowd in blouses and shirtsleeves stood outside the church. A knot of young men opened up as we approached; Tim's buddies from the ski academy squeezed his shoulders and hugged him.

Sun slanted through the stained glass and fell on the wooden pews. A balcony, nearing capacity thirty minutes before the service, hung above us. The first three rows on the main floor were reserved for family, and the rest were filling up quickly.

Kathy and Rick had lost their daughter, Debbie, to cancer in 1984. Afterwards, Kathy became a dedicated volunteer at the local hospice. Rick, a family physician, became the regional expert in palliative care. The church was full of their community; many were veteran grievers.

I walked downstairs and pretended to look at the art in the church basement—cross-stitch of a log cabin, watercolor of a sunset at the lake, child and kitten on a piece of tin.

Rick came by in the dim light. All week, he had been making arrangements, phone calls, visits, and rearrangements. He never stopped.

"Hi, Jenn," he said. "Did you find some people to sit with?"

I didn't say anything—that settled it. I wouldn't be sitting with the family.

"My dad just didn't know what people would think," Tim said later.

When upstairs got quiet, I slipped into a pew with two of my girlfriends from university. The family, along with Tim's closest friends from his skiing days, filed into the front rows, and the service began.

My friend put her arms around me, and I started to cry. Until then, I had only cried at night, after Tim and Rick went to bed. Those tears held a swirl of emotion. I cried for Tim and Rick, but I also, for the first time, allowed room for my own private sorrow. I had lost my friend Kathy— not Tim's mum or Rick's wife, but the woman I knew and loved. Her tiny smile, the silly voice she used to make us laugh, her unshakeable belief in healing energy. That was the sorrow that would be displaced in the months to come.

The rest of my tears came from a bruised sense of belonging. I had wanted to be included in the family circle, and I shocked myself with the pettiness of that; it embarrassed me.

✳

MOSQUITOES WHINED OUTSIDE the tent when I woke up the morning after our giant spaghetti dinner. I reached behind my head to undo the valve of my Therm-a-Rest, and then I remembered: rest day. No need to go anywhere. My mind turned to the idea of a proper bath.

I climbed from the tent to a scene that made my heart soar. Our camp huddled at a confluence of space and time. The wide, sandy banks of the Back River led downstream to our future, and the Baillie stretched back into our past. The third channel, which flowed from the Back's headwaters, marked a journey we would never know.

I followed a thin trail of smoke to a large rock behind which Levi and Drew had built the ultimate camp kitchen, complete with a flat rock and a cooking fire. Drew's twigs and driftwood treasures were paying off. Each day, he had loaded and unloaded the bundle wrapped in webbing. That morning, he coaxed a flame from the sticks, and Levi sat cross-legged frying pancakes.

A few feet away, Drew had done a masterful job of setting up our bug tent, and we were going to need it. He had used paddles, rocks, and guy lines to erect a tarp with long swathes of bug netting sewn around the edges of it. The tarp would keep off the worst of the wind and rain, but

A typical camp setup. CREDIT: LEVI WALDRON

with the mesh down it became a bug-free haven we couldn't do without. Jen sat inside with her mug of coffee.

I pulled some Campsuds biodegradable soap from the wannigan and headed down to the water, pulling my sweater over my head as I went. It must have been at least 12 or 15 degrees Celsius already. A welcome break from the cold that chapped my hands. I considered doing some laundry, which meant balancing a tricky equation. I would need a weather window when I didn't need the clothes and we'd be away from the water long enough for them to dry. I decided to limit my efforts to my underwear.

Reluctance to enter the water isn't an option with tundra mosquitoes hounding your flesh. It's best to have a good routine for bathing; the ideal is one smooth motion. Strip off your top and use it to swat mosquitoes as best you can while you yank off your bra, socks, pants, and underwear as quickly as possible. Throw your top to the beach, grab your underwear for laundering, take a deep breath, and go under. Never mind that the cold takes your breath away and blurs your vision. The bugs will stay off long enough to get the important spots—if you're quick.

I scrubbed my skin to suds with a dime-sized dab of soap, swished my undies around in the water, and scrabbled at my hair with dirty fingernails. Those actions completed my arrival in the tundra. The water pulled away the final remnants of the city and left my whole body burning with cold.

Back on shore, clammy and bug-bitten, I was hungry. Tim arrived with a prize from the barrel: a liter of maple butter straight from our friend's sugar bush back home. We slathered it over the pancakes and lay back against the rocks.

After breakfast, Levi, Alie, and Drew—the Swim Team— streaked to the river for some kung fu kicks and a dip. Jen started on cleanup. Tim and I took to the hills.

Sandy banks, left standing as the river cut deeper into the land, opened like gates, showing us the expanse of the Back—two city blocks across. Cushions of moss campion sprang from the sandy slopes in isolated clumps. Pinpoint buds in bright pink emerged among their greening leaves. High banks had dried, and the deep green of heather and Labrador tea rose over last week's brown. Sun. No more stranded ice.

The riverbank stood higher than a house. Smooth stones, glued together by sand, sloped down to the water on our right and drew a clean line against the sky on our left. The rising bank gave room for my thoughts to shift and breathe. When we finally crested the hill, we discovered a high plain—green, blue, and beige—that stretched to infinity. Bright water sliced across the canvas. A perfect breeze kept the bugs away.

We didn't have to speak to know that we would head upstream, away from the path of our canoes, but I thought we would talk about Tim's sadness from the previous night. I thought about asking that question: *Do you want to talk about it?* But it felt better just to walk.

Below us, two rivers cleaved the landscape. Their valleys were young and showed us erosion, spring flood, the river's tumble, and plants colonizing new soil. Above those excavations, the land lay still. Ribbons of eskers traced the glaciers' escape. When I looked down, I realized we were standing in the middle of a stone circle. A tent ring. Groups of nomadic Inuit would have lived along the banks of the river for thousands of years. Stones that held down the edges of summer tents made from caribou hide remain—often at beautiful, breezy lookout points. It's only in the last century that these families began moving toward settlements; the rings could have been hundreds of years old.

Farther upstream we lay down among the tiny mountain avens that were starting to bloom and took pictures of each other; my smile almost fills the frame. Later, I spotted a smudge of movement in the distance.

"Tim," I said, and he followed my gaze until he found it too.

That was the privilege of traveling with a friend who shared so much of my experience: a glance at the ground or wave to the horizon and Tim always knew what I had seen. We both smiled as the smudge resolved into a mother grizzly and cub.

On the way home we saw Drew and Jen, told them about the bears, and directed them to the tent rings. Farther along, Levi sat alone on a steep bank. We followed his gaze to a wolf cruising along the opposite bank. Our eleventh sighting in nine days: *Kathy*.

✳

OUR THREE CANOES dug into shore the next morning. The current pulled the sterns downstream; red spray decks stretched tightly over each and concealed our gear. Our camp had returned to a patch of tundra.

We clustered around Jen at the water's edge.

"I want to make an offering to the river," she said.

Jen held out a long piece of dried caribou with a white border of sinew. She bit a chunk from the meat and passed it around the circle. Levi passed. I was normally a vegetarian but wanted to participate. I took the leathery strip and tried to picture what part of the animal that ribbon had been cut from. It felt stiff in my hand but still alive—as if, were I to pour water on it, it would turn back into living flesh. I pushed my teeth into the muscle fibers, tore a piece off, and handed the meat to Drew. As I chewed, the sinew shrank to an elastic band and the taste of blood lined my mouth. Maybe that is the tundra's true flavor.

Jen tossed the remaining caribou into the current.

"For safe passage," she said, as the river pulled it under.

CHAPTER 5

NAMESAKE

P acking those strands of meat had been a trial. On our preparation day in Yellowknife, Jen had bounced in and announced, "I got the caribou."

The caribou? Then I remembered: she had ordered local caribou jerky. Jen, with her big grin and spiky blonde pigtails, held out a large canvas shopping bag that bulged with spikes of meat and sinew.

"Wow," I said, "it's bigger than I thought. We'll need more Ziplocs to pack it." I had been expecting a package of caribou pepperoni. How would we wrestle a shredded hindquarter into our overstuffed bags?

"We aren't supposed to put it in plastic; it needs to be exposed to the air so it doesn't go bad."

I looked up in disbelief. We had spent the day weatherproofing and bearproofing more than 300 kilograms (700 pounds to be exact) of vegetarian food, and our only meat was supposed to air-dry.

"It cost 120 bucks."

"It has to go in the packs," I said. "It'll get wet otherwise. And attract animals. Don't you think?" I tried to be diplomatic.

Jen and I had met in university, where I marveled at her super-active social life. She was also an expert at goal setting. As soon as Jen uttered, "I'd like to do this," it was as good as done: get a job in Toronto, buy a house (renovate it!), spend time in the North, take a big canoe trip. A partner and kids would come later. What she lacked in experience she made up for in efficiency; she acted fast. I could hardly keep up. No sooner did she finish her house than she moved out of it. No sooner did she start online dating, after the trip, than she fell in love and started a family. Why couldn't I make life move like that?

We found the rest of our plastic bags and bent as much of the meat into them as we could. I wondered about the white fibers that ran off the ends like nylon floss. We unpacked two of the barrels to bury some jerky and found corners in the other packs where we stuffed the rest of it.

TEN DAYS LATER we had barely touched the caribou, but we were starting to make a dent in the rest of our food, and our camp routines were coming together. We had solidified our cooking teams: Alie and me, Jen and Tim, and Levi and Drew. Once every three days, each pair took responsibility for all of the cooking and cleaning for one twenty-four-hour period, and then we got two days off to set up camp and hang out. Cooking in pairs was a habit for Tim, Levi, and me—a system we had grown to love. It meant lots of work when it was your day—organizing, prepping, and cooking three meals and snacks for six people, plus washing dishes—but we loved the free time it gave us on other days. Cooking pairs offset our paddling partnerships, except for Drew and Levi, who were double-paired because of our early switch.

Kitchen duty also meant locating all of the food for the next day. Our meticulously organized barrels should have made our next meal easy to find, but a bucket full of Ziploc bags is a slippery place. Everything got mixed up in a hurry.

We had packed 4,000 calories per person per day, which added up to about a kilogram of dry goods per person each day. Multiply by six people and fifty days, plus emergency rations, and we needed to pack and carry 320 kilograms (about 700 pounds) of food. None of us had a lot of money, so by drying our own food and looking for deals, we had assembled our rations for about six dollars per person per day. Drew built a dehydrator out of a cardboard box, a light bulb, and a small fan. He started experimenting and created tofu jerky (innovative, but not recommended). Tim, Levi, and I used our own dehydrators to dry soups, stews, burrito filling, salsa, and pizza toppings. Tim made vegetable leathers from yams and carrots. Jen and Alie packed dry goods. Someone hid jujubes in the pasta for an extra treat. I collected instructions for no-bake cookies, and Levi perfected our bannock recipe.

By June we had pulled together a large daily menu with a ten-day buffer. We brought fishing gear but wouldn't rely on it. Our barrels, wannigans, and canoe packs carried, among other things:

— 21 kilos of gorp (acronym for Good Old Raisins and
    Peanuts, but ours had lots of other ingredients too)
— 96 homemade granola bars

- 9 kilos of peanut butter, 6 of honey, 2 of jam, 1½ of almond butter
- 7 liters of oil, 4 of margarine, 1 of Nutella
- 150 cups of wheat flour, 40 of sugar, 20 of rice
- 15 kilos of pasta
- tahini, maple syrup, popcorn, quinoa, bulgur, soy sauce, vinegar, spice kit, chilies
- 18 packages of home-dried hummus and bean dip, 6 bags of dried pizza sauce
- 20 kilos of cheese

Some items, like balsamic vinegar and extra chocolate, seemed extravagant, but we knew that good food makes for strong memories and helps everyone get along. Some people are happy with a sack of rice and a fishing rod or a barrel full of freeze-dried tofu teriyaki and trail mix, but I am not one of them. Only jaw-dropping wildlife sightings and the adrenaline rush of perfectly navigating a rapid come close to the pleasure of sinking your teeth into fresh-baked cinnamon buns so far from the nearest town.

We did our best to pack the food logically in our barrels and packs. We spread cheese, honey, flour, fuel, and other items that would need replenishing throughout the stash. We filled four blue plastic barrels, then started on the packs. We lined each one with a homemade nylon sack, then with two heavyweight clear garbage bags to keep the smells in and the water out. I hoped that our advance sorting would keep us from opening more than two bags at mealtimes. As the packs grew in girth, we named each of them. The Orb of Joy looked disturbingly spherical. Blueberry Pie was the heaviest. With any luck, we would not join the long list of

people who had starved or nearly starved in the Arctic—
which included the river's namesake.

*

AS LIEUTENANT JOHN Franklin's midshipman between 1819
and 1822, George Back spent some desperate and hungry
months in Canada. It was Franklin's first overland expedition for the British Navy, and Back was twenty-two years
old when it started. By then, Back was accustomed to mag-
goty biscuits and stagnant water. He had been in the navy
half his life.

Back was born in England in 1796, when prospects
were poor for many children, even those of the middle
class. Girls worked long days in cotton mills or clothing
factories, and boys pulled carts down the damp shafts of
coal mines. There was no law limiting children's hours of
work until 1833. Life at sea—where children would receive
clothing, hot meals, a place to sleep, and some semblance
of education and medical care—didn't seem so bad. For
these reasons, and because of Back's childhood passion for
seafaring, his parents sent him off on his first ship in 1808,
during the Napoleonic wars. They would not see him again
for five years.

After only seven months with the navy, Back and some of
his shipmates were captured by French troops off the north
coast of Spain and sent to France, where Back lived in a
Napoleonic prison until 1814. It was more like house arrest
than a modern jail. Officers set up a school where Back
learned mathematics, navigation, and theories of seamanship,
as well as French and drawing—skills indispensable to an
Arctic explorer. The incarcerated men received money from

England for books, and they set up masts in town to practice rigging. Besides hunting, swimming, playing cricket,
and riding ponies, many prisoners drank heavily, gambled,
took mistresses or "women of pleasure" (over whom they
sometimes killed each other), and held kangaroo courts,
where the accused were beaten or humiliated. Back described
it as "Excess, no matter in what."[1] He was through most of
his teenage years by the time he returned to England to see
his family again.

After Napoleon's defeat, the British navy was cut from
150,000 men to 20,000. Only forty-six of the seven hundred
commanders had active jobs. John Barrow, the Admiralty's
second secretary, resolved to improve prospects for "the
boys" by sending them to explore the Canadian North.
Barrow planned to find a viable commercial route to the
Orient via the elusive Northwest Passage, and he would
create maps and celebrities in the process.

Once the machine got started, exploration became a
new route to fame. Parliament offered rewards for successful journeys. Returning commanders wrote books, sat for
portraits, and worked the lecture circuit. The best way to
get really famous was to disappear, as Franklin—by then
Sir John Franklin—would inadvertently prove.

Back was lucky to be appointed to Franklin's first overland expedition. He was lucky to have a job and lucky to
survive it. The expedition goes down as one of the navy's
most disastrous. The officers had no experience in overland
travel; they could not hunt and knew nothing about rivers,
canoes, the Arctic winter, or local politics. Some of Franklin's
first mistakes were related to food. On a tip from fellow
Englishman John Pritchard, Franklin started from England

with 350 kilograms (about 770 pounds) of salted pig for the men's rations, but it was already rotting and useless by the time they got to York Factory, on the shore of Hudson Bay. They replaced the pig with more traditional pemmican, a mix of powdered meat (usually bison), fat, and sometimes berries. It was a start, but there wasn't enough and they didn't have a good backup plan. More than two years into their journey, in the fall of 1821, John Franklin and his men ran out of food near the Arctic coast on what is now called the Hood River. They were far away from help.

Day by day, the men trudged south. They had a couple of minor hunting victories such as a small caribou (split twenty ways) and a couple of ptarmigan. Mostly, they ate curly black lichen, called tripe-de-roche, which gave them diarrhea. When they found a rotten caribou spine, they shared the marrow between them. The temperature dropped and the terrain grew more difficult. Men started to fall behind, and then they started to die. Franklin eventually sent some of the stronger men ahead (including Back), while the weaker ones did their best to carry on—but they didn't all make it to the shared camp, and some were never seen again. One of the men who disappeared was allegedly murdered, and another, Officer Hood, was found with a bullet through his head. After Hood's death, the survivors singed the hair off his buffalo robe and ate it. A couple of days later, Dr. Richardson, the expedition's surgeon and naturalist, exacted retribution by shooting Hood's accused murderer.

Only nine of Franklin's original team of twenty returned to England with him; from the Admiralty's point of view, however, the men had succeeded in running the Coppermine River to the ocean and mapping the coast heading east.

The journey took three years, during which Franklin traveled almost 9,000 kilometers. He returned to England a hero and received a promotion.

Back accompanied Franklin on his second overland expedition as well, but their relationship was rocky. Franklin complained about Back in private letters, though neither man's official journals describe any discord. The men had learned from the disasters of their first expedition together, and their journey along the Mackenzie River was more comfortable, but their relations deteriorated even further. Their interpersonal problems were likely a main reason Back did not go on Franklin's final and fatal mission to find the Northwest Passage in 1845.

IN FEBRUARY 1833, at age thirty-six, George Back left England on his third expedition to the Canadian Arctic. This time, the short, stocky explorer was in command. His objective was to reach the Arctic coast by a river called the Thlew-ee-choh, or Great Fish, which no one had ever run. Back's orders were to find it, descend it, and then search the coastline for a missing British expedition. Captain John Ross, along with his nephew James and twenty-two men, had not been heard from in four years. Back's second objective, failing a rescue, was to fill in a blank on the British map by heading west toward Point Turnagain—the last place Franklin and Back had reached from the mouth of the Coppermine in 1821.

Back hired several men in England, including Richard King, a naturalist and surgeon, who would be his second in command. He picked up the rest of his crew, including

Alexander McLeod, the expedition assistant, en route from New York to Great Slave Lake. He reached Great Slave in August and directed McLeod to find a wintering site and begin building Fort Reliance. Meanwhile, Back pressed on in search of the source of the mysterious Thlew-ee-choh. Although summer was nearing its end, the weather remained unusually warm—and that's where the problems began.

On August 22, McLeod and four men arrived at the bay where they would spend the winter. They began work atop a bank of gravel and sand; an abundance of mosses and shrubs surrounded the building site. Back said it was "more like a park than part of an American forest."[2] The men lost no time cutting suitable lumber for the walls and finding clay for the mortar. They erected three buildings out of squared logs, clay-mud, and wooden shingles. Each room had a fireplace with a granite chimney. Fort Reliance was taking shape.

Meanwhile, to the east, Back, along with his Dene guide, Maufelly, and a small party of men, continued toward the headwaters of the Thlew-ee-choh. The warm weather subjected everyone to late-season torment by biting flies, which made their faces bleed. According to Back, "There is certainly no form of wretchedness . . . at once so great and so humiliating, as the torture inflicted by these puny blood-suckers."[3]

By August 29, Back's team was drinking grog out on the tundra and celebrating their "discovery" of the headwaters. Planning to return in the spring to begin their descent toward the Arctic Coast, they turned back and headed toward Great Slave Lake.

The warm weather sped their return, but when hungry hunters started arriving, they realized that the warm spell was also changing the migration patterns of the caribou. The herds hadn't moved south to the tree line at the usual time; nor were they following their usual routes. Back wrote: "To this unusual mildness of the season may be ascribed the unparalleled sufferings of the Indians, who, emaciated and worn out by fatigue, continued to pour in upon us from the barren lands, where, contrary to their habits, the deer [caribou] still remained; keeping at too great a distance to be followed."[4]

It was normal for forts and trading posts to become hubs for local hunters, but the scene at Fort Reliance that year was different. People needed help. Back had winter provisions, but he'd planned to trade for more food. This strategy was common, though it had proved disastrous for past expeditions; trading plans were sure to fail in the midst of a widespread famine.

Elders, hunters, and families showed up hoping for scraps of pemmican. Instead, they were lucky to receive "A handful of mouldy pounded meat, which had been originally reserved for our dogs."[5] Some nights, Dene families would stand at the elbows of Back's men while they ate, watching each spoonful go into their mouths. Back sent his crew far afield to fish and hunt. He discharged a few paddlers and voyageurs to return south. And he reduced the portions of some of the native hunters so drastically that they were forced to leave in search of food.

The relationship between Back, his crew, and the local people was complicated. Back criticized and mistrusted the

Dene, but he also relied on them completely to find the river he sought. Although he did give out some of his food, especially to children, he couldn't, or wouldn't, feed everyone. Some Dene starved that winter, though Back's men all survived. Back felt he needed to save his large supply of pemmican for the following summer's river trip. Yet by Christmas he had already used half of it.

Darkness pressed against the moose-skin windows on Christmas evening. The temperature outside neared –60 degrees Celsius; inside, it wasn't much warmer. The fireplaces offered little comfort to the hungry explorers and starving families who waited for the holiday meal. For Back's men, Christmas dinner was a reduced ration of pemmican. Some of the children got a spoonful or two. For the others, it was nothing but a mouthful of their own caribou-hide clothing. While Back and his men swapped memories of balmy England, some of the local people cried out in their suffering. King, the surgeon, attended to those he could, but had little aid to offer. George Back sat quietly at the table. He wrote that "Happiness on such occasions depends entirely on the mood and temper of the individuals."[6] He and King considered opening their special tin of food, given to them by a woman in New York, but decided to wait until McLeod returned from a hunting trip. Instead, they dined on a small dish of pemmican, swapping stories about roast beef, plum pudding, and friends back home. With Back's determined cheer, which buoyed the others in his party, they managed to squeeze some Christmas joy from their grim situation.

The brutal winter conditions continued. The men saw few animals outside the fort, and punishing cold seeped through the logs day and night. The men conducted science experiments by observing the freezing points of everything around them. When Back splashed water on his face, droplets froze in his hair before he could wipe himself dry. Wounds opened on his hands when his skin cracked, and he tried to heal them with grease. He tried to work on his paintings by the fire, but his brush froze stiff.

Relief would not arrive until February 9, when Alexander McLeod returned with a hunting party and toboggans loaded with meat. Between his efforts and the sporadic success of other hunters, a trickle of food kept Fort Reliance going until spring.

✳

I SOMETIMES FELT embarrassed about the goodies we packed and the relatively elaborate recipes we enjoyed when I talked to some of the other guides and trippers I knew back home. Making your own tortillas, for example, might be going a little overboard. But we traveled the river from a position of privilege. We had lives that could accommodate two months away, and we had a bit of extra money to go beyond the demands of the day-to-day. I figured some extra chocolate chips and apricot jam—instead of a sack of beans—could only help, as long as our backs could take the weight.

CHAPTER 6

APPROACH

D rew had rolled up his pants, but they were wet anyway. The weight of the blue food barrel on his back had him bent almost double, and he was reaching for the painter line buried somewhere in the bow. Levi didn't bother to roll up his pants; he just stepped out into the shin-deep water, put his hands on his hips, and looked around. After a short exchange with Drew, Levi picked up a pack and they hauled the lines in unison.

The new river, after the confluence, engulfed us in a maze of dunes and meandering braids. Silt and sand obscured the river bottom and made it anybody's guess which channel would be deepest. Levi and Drew had guessed wrong. Once they hit bottom, the silty riverbed molded to their boat. The longer they sat, the deeper they sank. Nothing short of unloading themselves and half of their gear would free them, so they got out and searched for the deep channel on foot, dragging the sluggish canoe behind them. Drew found the channel by plunging in up to his thigh.

A few muskox munched away on shore as Alie and I rigged up a sail from two paddles and a small green tarp. The blaze of sun and the dry wind cracked my nose and mouth, and I tugged on my hat. Luck kept us in the deep channel, and we soared ahead of the others. I gazed past Alie's pigtails and her fleece-clad arms gripping the sail to watch the muskox in the distance. They had survived the winter by scraping through windblown snow to graze on vegetation so tough it would need several days to be digested. In summer, life is easier but much the same. Muskox stay in groups, leaning their shaggy faces into the wind. They watch for predators but don't run. They protect themselves from the circling wolves by forming a line or an outward-facing circle with curved horns jutting forward. On the sandy plains around that part of the Back, as wind whipped a film of sand into the air, the animals looked more like water buffalo from India than creatures native to the Arctic. The two species are from the same family, which includes cattle, goats, sheep, and antelope—but only one, called Oomingmak ("the bearded one") by the Inuit, has evolved to this life of extremes.

The flat expanse of sand challenged me mentally. I felt bored, though I was embarrassed to admit that, even to myself. *Will it be like this the whole time?* There was so much space, but I felt squeezed. And the sand itself overwhelmed me. It got into everything: the hood of my sleeping bag, the zipper on my coat, the bannock, the oil, the rim of my water bottle, my hair. The sand made me hate the things I thought I loved about the Arctic: the endless views, the scale, the uncaring weather. I wanted sunny periods and a gentle breeze instead of wind that battered our faces and cold that swelled our hands to uselessness.

After a long day in the dust bowl, I went to bed early. The tent offered sensory deprivation; its bland beige hid me from the searing light, bugs, wind, the others. I took off my socks to air out my itchy, swollen feet and opened my journal to the next blank page. A message in purple block letters in Dalton's handwriting screamed at me: "I'M THINKING OF YOU!" My throat tightened. That diary was my own private, empty space. How could he have opened it, blank or not? I resented his over-familiarity with my things. We had not made any promises; yet here he was, in my face.

Two weeks into the trip and I felt unsettled about how the experience was measuring up. I couldn't help making comparisons to my first Arctic summer on the Coppermine and Hood Rivers. That trip lived in my mind as a joyful romp. We'd had some tough days, but we'd also had fun; I remembered laughing a lot that summer. I was twenty-five years old and in love. My boyfriend at that time was a broad-shouldered wilderness guide from Saskatchewan with a knack for tracking grizzly and polar bears.

He had plenty of Arctic experience himself as an Arctic fox researcher, so when I told him about the canoe trip, he understood, and he sent me North with two things. The first was a package of tiny letters handwritten on photocopied topographical maps. Each one was folded down to 2 inches square, marked with the day I was supposed to open it and sealed with packing tape to make it waterproof. The letters hardly took any space; they asserted his presence yet allowed me my freedom. My pulse quickened each time I opened one. I cherished the letters; they were incredibly sweet, but despite their assertions, home became more and more distant as the days wore on.

The second gift was a ring he had carved by hand from caribou antler. A thin, polished circle that fit perfectly. I knew it was foolish, but I wore it on the trip, even when my fingers swelled from cold and wind. During a storm one night, early in the trip, the pegs holding down my tent's vestibule pulled out of the ground. The wet fly slapped at our door, soaking the tent and making a racket. I opened the tent door, and while the rain lashed my face, I reached out with the edge of the fly in my hand to force it back into the ground. As I drove my hand down on the metal peg, it connected with the ring and smashed it into three pieces. I lay on my stomach, half out of the tent and exposed to a driving wind, and looked at the fragments in shock. It was hard to hold on to home out there.

On the Back, part of me wanted to let go of everything and imagine that life on the river was my only life, but I struggled to find my rhythm. I worried about Tim, and I still felt distant from Jen, Drew, and Alie. I expected the tundra to clear the cobwebs, turn on the creativity, dispense with my worries, and strengthen my body. I wanted it to do the work for me. Perhaps I was becoming one of those people who ask too much of the wilderness, who cram it so full of expectations that it becomes more of an idea than a real place. I was tired of reading about the wilderness as a backdrop for so-and-so's personal struggle; yet there I was, dragging my anxieties across the North. I longed to be my best self and was afraid that person wouldn't show up.

To calm myself, I decided to organize something, a tactic that usually works. I turned to my packing list. There were certain things I didn't want to forget for next time, like how my underwear line was digging into my backside day after day while I knelt in the boat.

— *Underwear—3 pairs with different panty lines! (1 cotton, 1 polypro or something, 1 other)*
— *Socks—liner socks, neoprene socks, wet socks (preferably high and bug-proof), dry socks (definitely high, thick, loose, and bug-proof)*

I should have brought a bandana to wipe my nose. A down jacket was much better than a down vest. Long underwear tops must have a high neck to keep bugs off.

I also dreamed about my future that night. I wanted to start a school that taught bush craft and all the practical skills of a simple life that are trickling away. I imagined writing books, especially about food for a trip, and paddling in manageable places, like Algonquin Park, near my hometown. In my mind, I slipped over the side of the boat and felt the kiss of warm water. I lay naked on warm rocks and ate fresh fruit.

Before sleep, I chastised myself: *Stop imagining yourself away. Be here; it's only week two.*

THE NEXT NIGHT, it was my turn to share a tent with Levi, and we lay beside each other as the wind pressed the fly into the tent ceiling and drizzle speared the nylon.

"This is one of those nights I feel especially grateful for our tents and sleeping bags," Levi said.

I smiled to myself and immediately split open my dry, cracked lip. "Me too."

"Do you remember Bob Dannert's weather system?" he asked. We had met Bob three years before in Bathurst Inlet and been impressed by his extensive CV of solo paddling.

"No."

"Shit, Shit Squared, and Shit Cubed. Shit weather is wind, rain, or cold. Shit Squared is two out of three. He said you never paddle in Shit Cubed."

We slept soundly and woke early to the same pressure on the fly. The tent felt dank and small.

I unzipped the door to a blast of cold air and rain. I could barely see into the mist. Shit Cubed.

I longed to fall back to sleep, but it was my turn to be Leader of the Day and therefore to assess the weather. The Leader of the Day was Alie's idea, and it helped to cut down on the time spent making group decisions. Rather than relying on consensus (endless) or majority (divisive) we took turns bearing responsibility for the final call. The Leader of the Day's job was to gather information, canvass opinions, and lead discussions. The final decision on everyday things like when to stop and where to have lunch was the burden and privilege of the Leader of the Day. By rotating the position equally, we all got a turn in the hot seat, which made it harder to criticize others and carried a built-in incentive to go easy on them; it would always be your turn soon enough. Leader of the Day provided a structure that complemented our paddling and cooking teams, and we also took turns as Navigator of the Day to share the map work. Clearly assigned roles helped off-duty times feel more free, so we still had room for the people we bonded with easily: Jen and Drew made each other laugh; Tim and I talked a lot. New friendships were developing too: Drew asked Tim about wildlife; Alie and Levi lounged by the water.

That day the decision to stay in camp was easy. Paddling would have been nearly impossible, so I let everyone sleep and headed to the food barrels. If we were weather-bound, we had enough time for cinnamon buns, and Alie and I were on kitchen duty that day. I unsnapped the lid of the baking barrel and found the basics for making bannock dough. I was careful to block the bags from the wind and rain as best I could. Huddled behind an overturned canoe, I poured river water into the flour mixture and squished it together by hand. Little flecks of dirt from my nails blended in. I grabbed a water bottle for a rolling pin and dropped the dough onto the wannigan lid. I tugged and tore the dough, patched it up, rolled it, and stretched it again until it covered the lid. I slathered margarine as thick as peanut butter on bread. Then I spread sugar, spices, and raisins on the dough and rolled it into a thick log. I sliced it into rounds and nestled them into the frying pan. A lid and insulating hood turned our frying pan into an oven. I hoped the buns would rise a little.

Alie soon joined me and began her morning coffee ritual. I hadn't seen Alie in a few years when she and Jen met the rest of us at the Yellowknife bus station after our twenty-four-hour Greyhound marathon. She had flown in. She wore rugged sandals, a skirt, a cotton jersey shirt with a boat neck, and a silver ball-and-chain necklace tight to her throat. One pin held back a curl of ear-length brown hair. Alie had lots of lake and swift-water experience from a previous Arctic trip and had done lots of southern paddling, so she was no stranger to camping. But she also read books like *Anna Karenina* and enjoyed them. She was already a published poet, and her first novel would be released that fall. Back home, Alie and her friends congregated at a family cabin called The Beaver, where they bonded over food, dancing, and deep conversations about life—clothing optional. I squirmed thinking about this group intimacy; I had never been to a women's gathering. Alie's necklace summed her up for me: tough *and* feminine.

She was both easy and hard for me to talk to. When we paddled, I loved chatting about any subject, and she usually had ideas that led to an in-depth exchange. I told her about my parents and my love life. We wrote a song about rivers together and taught it to the others. But when Alie and I cooked or worked together, I felt awkward and distant from her. Procedures became confrontations, somehow, and I grew defensive. I tried to discuss kitchen setup or cooking ideas, but it often came out like a challenge instead of an olive branch. *She's made up her mind about me*, I worried. It didn't help that Alie often seemed tired and liked to sleep; I didn't want to keep her up after supper and make things worse.

As Alie carefully spooned the day's ration of grounds into her special mug, I dug for some granola, up to my elbow in pancake mix. I pulled a bag from the depths in victory and saw that it had one of Alie's handwritten quotations in with it. She had buried several in with our stores. The quotation read, "Task: to be where I am. Even when I'm in this solemn and absurd role: I am still the place where creation works on itself. —Tomas Tranströmer."[1]

The others quickly answered our calls of "Breakfast!" The buns bubbled and snapped in their oily pan, and six sets of grubby hands pulled at the stretchy dough. In our haste we burned our mouths. When the feast was over, we searched the moss for dropped raisins and ate them too.

＊

OVER THE NEXT few days the big lakes dominated our group talks. The wind had been growing during the afternoons and had reached a point where it sometimes stopped us, and always slowed us. If the trend continued, we would be wind-bound on shore and fall behind on the schedule we had established. Once we reached the lakes, which stretched for over 200 kilometers, it would only get worse and could become dangerous. Alie suggested we switch to an evening paddling schedule to avoid the wind as much as possible. We could hike and explore in the morning, eat our big meal at noon, and then leave camp with our lunch packed for an evening snack. We decided to give it a try. It was a sensible thing to do. I didn't think it would throw me that much.

During the first day of our new schedule, Jen was unusually quiet. She and Drew liked to joke around in the mornings by making faces and putting on weird voices, silly stuff, but she wasn't into it that day. On the water, she liked to sing, and sometimes she would get us to sing with her. At times it drove me insane—I didn't come out to the tundra to listen to someone belt out campfire songs—but that was on my bad days. I admired her for it too; she could be cheery when the landscape wasn't. One day, she sang me every song from *Hello, Dolly!*, which she had recently performed in. At first I loved it, then hated it, then laughed in disbelief that she was still singing an hour later. That afternoon, she broke her reliable paddling rhythm to look back at me.

"Fifty days is a lot," she said. "It seems like a lot." She gazed out across the endless water. From here to the ocean and then on forever.

"My hands are getting worse," she added.

She turned around again and spread her hands out on the red canvas spray deck. I climbed out of my seat and crawled forward. The backs of her hands were rough and chapped. Each finger was swollen out of proportion, so she could hardly straighten her fingers. The blisters had been spreading. At first there were only a few, but now they bloomed over each finger and each knuckle.

"I think it's the sun," she said. "I try to keep them covered, but my hands get cold in wet gloves."

"Ouch," was all I could think to say.

I'm pretty sure there were tears in her eyes as she turned back to the front and gripped her paddle again.

My hands were doing okay, but my feet had started to make me hobble. Long days in cold, wet shoes were taking their toll. My feet took ages to warm up each night, and they itched and burned during the day. Raised red welts crowned each toe joint, and red slices through the skin behind my toes were widening. Pools of blood sagged in the skin, making the soles dark and puffy. My toes moved slowly and cooled my fingers when I grabbed them. When I let go, they stayed white as I counted slowly to ten. The skin had become translucent and delicate. The opposite of what I needed.

Tim had lapsed into quiet too, and his face looked heavy. All of us seemed to carry a burden as we pulled ourselves toward the lakes. It was like living in a world where you don't exist, where nothing you do affects your environment. The land can neither see nor feel you. The lack of emotion in the outer world made the inner world more oppressive.

CHAPTER 7

LIBRARY

The evening schedule gave us enough relief from the daytime winds that we stuck with it. The main benefit of this change, according to me, was eating hot muffins for breakfast. Usually we had to cook them the night before, but now we had lots of time to make them when we got up. I tried to be gracious about the long mornings, the big lunches, and the endless night paddles, but I didn't do a very good job. For some reason that eluded me, night paddling made me incredibly cranky. Theoretically, we still had time to explore in the mornings, but it never felt relaxed. Departure would hang over my head, and the others would keep referring to their watches to plan the day. That drove me nuts. I wanted to forget about the hands on the clock, at least sometimes, and pay attention to natural cues of light and weather—or at least try.

I would mutter under my breath, "Didn't we come here to get away from a schedule?" or, "Careful, we might be *late*." I hated my mysterious bitterness but couldn't seem to shake it. Sometimes Tim would shoot me a warning look or hiss "*Take it easy*" under his breath.

"Don't be crazy," he said to me one night. "People are going to think you're too intense." We both knew it was true sometimes. On a previous trip, we had decided which fruit all of the paddlers were most like. Tim and Levi were apples—shiny, accessible, dependable—and I was a pineapple, good once you got past the spiky skin.

Once everyone had grown comfy with the new schedule, the wind died completely and the temperature soared. We would paddle until midnight some nights, and I would still wake at six or seven while everyone else slept. I had always been terrible at sleeping in. Alie was the most prodigious sleeper of all of us, and the later we paddled, the more I resented her for it. On the rare occasion that I did get some extra rest, I woke drenched in sweat under the midmorning sun. The heat forced me out, only for me to be attacked by mosquitoes, which had finally hatched en masse. I slapped them out of my ears until my bug jacket was on and then scowled at the silent tents.

Despite myself, during our free time I kept writing letters to Dalton in my journal. I described everything, reminisced, and made promises that were easy to write down so far away from home. On the river I could suspend my life, except for one detail: it had been several weeks since my last period, and I feared that one careless night would tie me to him forever.

ON THE MAP, the dreaded lakes looked like moths with shaggy wings that spread north and south. By the time we got there, the river was so wide we weren't sure exactly when we'd arrived. It took a day for us to be certain of our location, and we had to keep the map out constantly to keep track of the bays that would trap us in a dead end. The Garry Lakes sit in a black hole of Canadian geography, nowhere near any landmarks known to southerners, such as Hudson Bay, the Arctic coast, or the border between the Northwest Territories and Nunavut. A height of land north of the lakes marks a boundary beyond which dozens of rivers flow relatively straight into the Queen Maud Gulf. The Back flattens into an east-west line with very little elevation change. It's the heart of the tundra. Water rules the landscape.

We camped on an island near the north shore of Upper Garry Lake, the second lake in the series of seven. We had another hot morning, and the midmorning sun threw shadows behind each stone and gave a metallic sheen to the land. The air had warmed enough to allow us to wear just two shirts, and the lake reflected wisps of cloud and blue. A few mosquitoes whined, and small blossoms of yellow, pink, and white leapt out like stars from the sky: snow cinquefoil, moss campion, Labrador tea, blueberries, cloudberries, three-toothed saxifrage.

For a morning adventure, we walked to a cabin that sat alone in the distance. Its shell of thin boards had been burned dark and blackened by sun and cold. A rectangle with a slanted roof was tacked onto a simple square room with a peaked roof and one chimney—a cabin from a child's drawing. Shreds of tar paper clung to the outside.

We snapped a few photos and circled the little building. Beyond the front door, the green tundra gave way to pebbles as it sloped gently to the lake. Behind us, beyond our camp, a tall gravel ridge left by glacial river sediment rose and snaked away.

The inside of the cabin was bare except for the occasional board and some lemming scat. A book lay propped up against one wall: *The Man Who Mapped the Arctic: The Intrepid Life of George Back, Franklin's Lieutenant*, by Peter Steele.

Alie walked over and picked it up.

The inside front cover had been inscribed in black ballpoint pen: "July 10, 2005. YMCA Camp Widjiwagan Voyaguer [sic] girls of 2005." Next was a short request followed by seven signatures: "If you take this book, please leave another."

In Yellowknife, we had heard of a group of young women from a camp in Minnesota who had flown in shortly before us. They were headed for the ocean too. I knew that senior campers sometimes took long northern journeys, a modern coming-of-age ritual, but my mum and I spent summers at the cottage, so I could only imagine the traditions these girls might have. Had they already known each other? Who was their leader? It puzzled me to see seven names, because canoeists almost always travel two per boat. That meant that at least one of them didn't sign, or that someone was traveling solo or sitting in the middle of the canoe, maybe on a pack. I didn't envy the three-person boat, if there was one.

These girls had been in the cabin two days before we arrived. We could overtake them at some point, or they might pull away from us. I wondered if they felt small out there, if they sang enough camp songs to shield themselves from the silence.

Alie picked up the book and replaced it with her copy of *War and Peace*.

*

IN AUGUST OF 1949, a floatplane buzzed low over the north shore of Upper Garry Lake. It banked, descended to the water, and skipped to a stop by a small island. A skinny man wearing thick glasses climbed out and stepped onto the tundra. The island would be his new home. He was Father Joseph Buliard of the Missionary Oblates of Mary Immaculate, and he was there to establish Canada's most remote mission. That much he knew. What he didn't know was that within ten years, as a result of forces set in motion by his arrival, this land would be emptied of its people, and he would be gone too.

Buliard was born and raised in France, and he felt drawn to the most difficult missionary assignments from a young age. His first desire was to work among the Inuit of northern Canada, and by the time he reached the Garry Lakes, at age thirty-five, he'd already been in the Arctic for a decade. He'd served as a priest in the remote settlements of Repulse Bay and Baker Lake, on the north and west sides of Hudson Bay, ministering to Inuit around the Hudson Bay Company posts there. In each of those places, he experienced something that would shape the rest of his life.

Repulse Bay was his first post, and he arrived in September of 1939. On the morning of November 6, it was −30 degrees Celsius when he walked out across the sea ice by himself in search of game. Five kilometers away from the mission, he fell through the ice. By a slim chance— a miracle, in his mind—he managed to grip the ice edge and haul himself out, but his hands were badly frozen. After the rest of his body recovered, Buliard's hands oozed and

Father Joseph Buliard's cabin on Upper Garry Lake. CREDIT: JENNIFER KINGSLEY

gangrene threatened to set in. Because of bad weather, it took a month to get him to a proper hospital, where his hands were saved, but they remained swollen, painful, and highly sensitive to cold for the rest of his life. This accident only strengthened his resolve: "My enthusiasm is intact and if at all possible the Eskimos will see me back amongst them and I will spend my life for them willingly!"[1]

On his next posting, to Baker Lake, he encountered another force that would deeply affect him: the Protestants. Most of the Inuit in the area who considered themselves Christians were Anglicans, and their priest was Reverend

William John Rundle James, or simply Mister James. The Protestant hold over the Baker Lake region troubled Buliard and motivated him to travel deeper and deeper into the tundra in search of souls to save.

Buliard wanted to establish his own mission, and according to his biographer, he considered the "Back River as his own special battlefield, its only purpose being to convert pagan souls or those caught in heresy, no matter the obstacles: cold, hunger, weariness, mockery."[2] In the summer of 1949, he erected Our Lady of the Rosary Mission on a small island. He had visited the area before by dogsled and knew that the north shores of those lakes were home to about fifteen families of nomadic caribou-hunting Inuit.[3] The island was their summer gathering place. From there, he would bring them the word of the Lord.

Buliard spent summers working around the mission and gathering food for winter. When winter arrived, the priest—guided by local Inuit without whom he couldn't have survived—repeatedly traveled hundreds of kilometers by dogsled to visit the four hundred people living in small groups throughout the region. For four years, with occasional trips off-site or visits from other clergy, Buliard pushed himself to the limit to turn the Inuit away from their traditional beliefs and toward baptism and Christian prayer. It was a time of huge transition: missions were reaching farther across the tundra, residential schools were being established in the north, and tuberculosis was infecting people in remote communities.

Early in 1953, Buliard's life altered again when Anthony Manernaluk, a fifteen-year-old whose parents had died of TB, came to live with him at the mission. Manernaluk became Buliard's guide and companion; he kept the priest's mitts and boots clean of snow, hunted and fished, and built igloos when they traveled together. He helped compensate for Buliard's terrible eyesight, clumsy hands, and relative inexperience. The duo continued to travel in search of families on the move. They met people such as Ninayok and her husband, Sabgut, and hunters like the man Arnadjuak.[4] And of course, people also came to see Buliard at his cabin.

At least some of the Inuit held Buliard in high regard. And in his own way, Buliard cared about them. But he never learned to appreciate the Inuit's sophisticated concept of "nuna"—an Inuktitut word that encompasses the land and all of its biological and spiritual relationships. Buliard could not acknowledge the Inuit lifestyle without yearning to change it. In a letter home to France, he put it this way: "When one has seen the Inuit living like animals and now sees them behaving like saints, how could there remain any doubt about the effectiveness of your prayers and sacrifices?"[5]

No matter what Buliard may have thought of them, as time went on, people around the island came to him more and more frequently. He had supplies. Manernaluk and others taught the priest some of their skills, changing his relationship with the land; Buliard's missionary work did the same for them. His presence—especially his reliable supply of tea, ammunition, and relief rations—drew people to the island. In just a few years, families who'd survived entirely on wild foods, mainly caribou, began integrating Buliard's provisions into their subsistence economy. Soon, some of the local Inuit, like John Adjuk and his wife, stuck close to the mission. They had come to depend on it.

Then, on October 24, 1956, seven years after Buliard's arrival, everything at the Garry Lake mission suddenly changed. Buliard, by then forty-two years old, hitched up his dog team, planning to head a few miles onto the frozen lake to check his fishnets. As his clumsy hands set up the harnesses, Adjuk came over and expressed concern. Buliard's helper, Manernaluk, had been sent south to be treated for TB, so the priest was going out alone. Adjuk warned him that a storm was coming.

Buliard left anyway. The bad weather set in, and later five of his dogs returned to the mission. There was no sled with them and no priest. Adjuk went searching, but the blizzard had obliterated any tracks. Buliard's nets were untouched. He was never seen again.

That night remains a mystery. Did his bad eyesight lead him astray? Did he plunge through a thin patch of ice? The RCMP launched a brief murder investigation, but no one was ever charged. Everyone around the mission, for the most part, accepted his disappearance. Manernaluk, though, was deeply saddened. "When I heard of Father Buliard being lost," he said, "I felt I lost a parent."[6]

Officials in Baker Lake, nearly 300 kilometers southeast, didn't get word of Buliard's disappearance until January 1957. The news had been passed from the Garry Lake Inuit to missionaries farther north, then down to the RCMP in Churchill, and finally to Baker Lake. In June, Father Ernest Trinel was flown in to replace him. Caribou were sparse at the time, and some families were struggling, so Trinel picked up where Buliard had left off and gave out relief supplies. But this act would become highly controversial.

Distributing food and gear was a common practice at Arctic missions; it was part of their religious charity. But it also drew people to men who were trying to convert them, and that didn't sit well with some government officials. By the time Trinel arrived at Garry Lake, the federal government was encouraging a policy of increasing Inuit "independence"; the supplies were considered food aid and should only be used if the government deemed them necessary. That in itself was a problem; officials knew very little about life on the tundra and could often go months without getting any information about local residents.

In August of 1957, after two months at the mission, Trinel sent a message to Baker Lake: "A community of 60 Eskimos menaced to starve at Garry Lake."[7] The caribou had not come, and Trinel saw the situation as life-or-death. Government agents came in with a relief shipment in August and again in September. The nearby storehouse was stockpiled with food, and Manernaluk and others were put in charge of distributing it, but not everyone agreed that the rations were needed. Douglas Wilkinson, the Northern Affairs officer based in Baker Lake, called the food drop "the worst thing that could happen." He claimed the Inuit had "hoodwinked the father into giving out most of his supplies."[8] Meanwhile, Trinel was worried he himself wouldn't survive the winter. He left for Baker Lake in early December. On December 15, a final shipment of food arrived at the storehouse.

That winter was cold and grim. The lack of caribou meant people were not just hungry, but also poorly clothed. The government had given out fishnets, but they didn't do much good. It was another example of the government's ignorance about life on the land; a person cannot venture very far to fish in the middle of winter if he doesn't have proper clothing to keep him warm. Ninayok and Sabgut had put up lots of fish in the fall but had given them away to people who were even worse off than they were. A man named Angeelik shot nine caribou, but they were soon consumed. By early in the New Year, Ninayok told an official, "all the Eskimos were forced to eat their dogs."9

The situation became desperate in January and fatal by February. With barely any food left, starving and freezing, Arnadjuak and a companion traveled from their camp to the storehouse to see if they could gather supplies. Inside, they started a small stove. It exploded, and both men ran out into the cold. As the building burned, Arnadjuak ran to a nearby structure, crawled between two mattresses and died. His companion made it back to camp, but he had none of the food his family was expecting. It wasn't long before they all died of starvation.

Between late February and early March, a total of seventeen people died in the Back River region. One man was found frozen next to a fishing hole. The RCMP was responsible for making a winter patrol through the area, but did not do so. Father Trinel and government officials didn't make contact with Garry Lake until April 24. On May 10, Ninayok, who played an important role in piecing the story together, was evacuated for emergency medical treatment.

A flurry of government and media attention followed, placing blame all around. Some accounts held the Inuit responsible; others tried to blame the caribou for not showing up. Nobody wanted to assume responsibility: not the missions, for their role in altering the area's subsistence economy; not the government, for its ever-shifting relief policies; and not the police, for having failed to make their winter rounds. Some pointed to the storehouse fire as a single, clear cause, but a pathologist's report on the deaths cited prolonged starvation and exposure: "definite evidence of severe malnutrition as evidenced by weight loss and extreme loss of all fat from the body."[10]

After these events, the Department of Northern Affairs flew into action. Within five months they'd launched a dramatic project. They deployed staff to the Hudson Bay coast to choose a location for a new town. The site was recommended by civil servants from the south during an afternoon charter flight. A social worker tasked with comparing two sites wrote, "Relying only on my own unprofessional and superficial knowledge of the hydrography and geography of both areas I consider the Whale Cove site to be superior."[11] And so it was done. Some 500 kilometers from their homeland, a settlement for some of the survivors was built. The community was a conglomerate of Inuit speaking different dialects from different areas of the Northwest Territories and Nunavut, some of whom—including those from Garry Lake—had never seen the sea. Over the next year, the remaining Inuit from the Garry Lake area were relocated to a variety of camps and relocation projects. In some places, families were given 240-square-foot insulated plywood cabins. In others, they were reported as "living the traditional life,"[12] which meant tents and snow houses. The idea was to let Inuit people live independent lives.

The incoherence of the relocations is outlined in detail by Frank James Tester and Peter Kulchyski in their excellent book *Tammarniit (Mistakes)*. As they say, "The idea that

Inuit would be working with 'freedom from undue interference,' given the phenomenal plans being made for them, is more than ironic." Government documents revealed plans to unveil, "for the first time in the Arctic,"[13] a system in which Inuit would have to work in order to eat—never mind that they had been doing so for millennia.

It's shocking how quickly this all took place. By 1959, just a decade after Father Buliard had set up the first-ever mission at Garry Lake, nobody was left. The people from Garry Lake had either died or been moved away, but the cabin stubbornly remained.

✳

WE STASHED THE book in a pack and carried on across the lake. The sun approached the horizon slowly throughout the afternoon until the blue lake shifted toward silver. At the end of Upper Garry Lake, Levi dug some couscous salad out of the lunch bucket, and I ate mine with two willow twigs. Jen snapped a photo of my grubby grin and the yellow sky behind me. Then the current picked up and dropped us to the next lake, where Buliard faded to memory.

CHAPTER 8

STORM

L evi's barometer stayed sky-high as the lakes ticked past in a glassy calm. The water reflected the sky so perfectly that we seemed to be floating in a sphere of blue. The beauty lifted our spirits, and we alternated between reverent silence and silliness.

Around midnight, Tim stood in the stern of his canoe and steered while Drew powered the bow forward. "Manicotti!" Tim yelled.

We all turned and stared.

"Rigatoni! Cannelloni! Lasagna!" Tim held his paddle in the air above his head.

"I know all the pasta!" he cried in a terrible Italian accent.

Drew egged him on: "Penne!"

"Fusilli!"

"Macaroni!"

The tundra can make you manic, but for that evening Tim had shaken his grief, and that was enough to keep us going a little longer.

✳

THE MORNING BROUGHT continued calm, though the barometer had started to dip. We kept our eyes trained ahead, until the horizon line started to blur. The edge of the world became hazy, and then little pieces of ice started floating by.

Drew looked back and then looked forward again. "Um..."

Slowly, the thickness of the horizon resolved into a long gray band and then a silver sheet. As far as we could see, Lower Garry Lake was frozen solid.

Levi eventually broke the silence. "Let's get up high and take a look at this."

A small rock outcrop gave us some vantage. We scrambled to the top and huddled around the highest rock, which was about the size of a dining room table. Tim and Jen sat down, while Alie studied the map and Levi scanned with Tim's binoculars. Drew snapped some shots, and I shoved my hands into my pockets, incredulous. I had never been so surprised by something that, in retrospect, was unsurprising. *We should have planned for this,* I thought, but we hadn't.

"I wonder what it's like on the south shore," Alie said. We had been hugging the north edge of the lake. Perhaps the wind had pushed the ice up here, and the south side was clear.

"We could try it," I said.

"It's 20 k to get down there, and no guarantees," said Tim.

"Looks like there's a gap between the shore and the ice," Jen offered. "What about that?"

I took the map from Alie and reviewed where we were on the lake. The ice could go on for 50 kilometers for all we knew.

"I don't suppose waiting is an option?" I asked. Levi just looked at me. "Let's camp," I said.

We spent that evening weighing our options while surrounded by the brightness of the ice. Heading to the south shore could work, but it would mean at least an extra day, and it might be for nothing. Waiting was unrealistic. Portaging would be incredibly arduous. Picking our way between the ice and shore would be slow but safe, though we didn't know when the ice would close in, and then we'd be surrounded. The longer we talked, the more it came back to walking. We would have to walk across the ice. Precisely what every Canadian child is told never, ever to do.

The situation reminded me of the movie *Never Cry Wolf*. My parents took me to see it when I was six years old, not realizing how much it would terrify me. The main character, grasping his gun, falls through the ice. The current pulls him away from the hole, and he's left pounding up from underneath. The camera follows him underwater through a chaos of bubbles, then cuts to the surface where the forest stands neutral and silent.

THE NEXT MORNING we met for granola and the morning workout of getting our wet suits on. We planned to paddle until we couldn't and then work like dog teams to haul our cargo across the ice. We had no idea how long this would take.

I secured my damp wet suit around my ankles and began rolling it up my bare legs as mosquitoes chomped on my exposed thighs. A light wool shirt would protect my trunk and shoulders from the irritation of the neoprene, but my legs started to prickle immediately. *This could be a long day.*

"Let the quest for the Northeast Passage begin!" Drew cried.

We paddled over to the gap between ice and shore. Small pieces clacked against our hulls, and soon we were shoving small bergs aside with our paddles. As the pieces got bigger, we rammed them out of the way and kicked off from shore when necessary. I had anticipated thinner ice that sat on top of the water, like back home, but this stuff floated several inches above the surface and drooped an arm's length below. As we pushed and kicked our way through the ice, which was still floating, we got used to its weight and character. After 7 kilometers, the channels and gaps closed in. Time to walk.

"Seems pretty solid," said Tim as he tested his weight on it.

Each bow person carefully got out, grabbed the bow line, and hauled in as the stern paddler churned a couple more strokes before reaching a leg out and climbing onto the ice. It had a clear layer on top that looked like bubble wrap and popped as we walked across it. Levi and I had *Bluebell*, our longest boat. I was reluctant to leave her side. Shallow pools littered the ice surface, but it felt solid enough beneath my running shoes. Levi grabbed the bow line; I grabbed the stern line. We leaned into the ropes and felt her begin to slide.

Within minutes, sweat prickled into my suit and my back began to ache.

Jen and Drew drag their canoe across kilometers of ice. CREDIT: LEVI WALDRON

"We can't do this all day," I said. Then my foot broke through a patch of gray ice, and I dropped to my knees.

We tried different rope lengths, front and back, side by side. We tied the ropes up by our shoulders and down at our waists. A good lean forward and small steps helped, but the boats still weighed a few hundred pounds. After a while, Levi found the winning system. He tied the bow line to the middle of a paddle, and we pushed against it—one on each side of the rope—in unison. We moved ahead with short steps and tried to stay on the white ice; the gray stuff would swallow our feet. We jumped small channels, learned to cling to our boats when the ice got rotten, and invented smooth bobsled-like transitions to cross small pools.

"This is getting fun," said Tim.

After a slow 4 kilometers, we stopped for lunch. Drew stripped down to his waist. His orange chest hair moved in the breeze as he paced the ice with a chunk of Gouda cheese in his hand. Despite the ice, we were sweating profusely, and the mosquitoes had found us. Even out on a huge frozen lake, escape was impossible; if they could find us out there, they could find us anywhere.

I walked away from the group to take a pee. I was out in the open, but privacy was mostly forgotten by then. I peeled the top of my wet suit down to my waist, and steam rose to my face. When I released myself from the neoprene and squatted, a hot rush of blood splattered on the ice. It melted the surface and made a tiny pool. Relief washed through me at the sight of the blood, and I felt a thin cord break between me and my life at home.

The landscape did not change all day. Morsels of ice collided in the intermittent pools of open water and filled the air with their tinkling. The drag of our boats provided a constant background hum as the ice scoured and scrubbed us with each step. Drew and Jen balanced their boat across a gap in the ice for a photo, and Levi lay on his belly for some close-up ice shots. I posed with one leg on either side of a wide crack. Drew went in up to his armpits once, and so did I.

The stubborn irritations that had been bothering me began to recede. The sweat against my body and aching muscles helped to work them out. The enormity of the ice shifted my perspective too; my frustrations with the schedule and my worries about the group didn't seem like such a big deal when compared to the task at hand. We all felt the cleansing; what had been so uncertain at the beginning of the day now seemed like an adventure. Annoyances simply let go—as if they couldn't make it across the ice.

By late afternoon, the white ice lost some of its shine, and rotten gray ice transitioned to bigger and bigger pools of open water. With a paddle-swirling flourish we arrived back in our preferred medium: water. We hooted in triumph, and the air felt clear of any tension or sorrow.

The journey was set to begin again, but if I wanted a fresh start, I had one more thing to take care of.

I walked away from camp that night toward a rise of land in the distance. From the top, I scanned the landscape once more, inch by inch, for caribou. I turned around twice, searching each bump and stone for signs of life.

"It's okay," I said to the air. "It's okay. Thank you anyway."

My desire to find that herd of caribou had become a distraction. It was time to let go.

That night, the barometer continued to drop.

BY 7:30 THE next morning, we had packed up the boats. The wind rose quickly, but we were anxious to leave our wet campsite, which was covered in goose droppings. Our location was relatively protected, so the wind didn't force the water into waves but skittered across its surface like sheets of rain. It pressed against the blade of my paddle at every recovery stroke and flattened my jacket to my chest. By the time we had crossed to the first set of nearby islands—mere rock piles between us and the main shore— the wind had overpowered Levi and Jen, and they lost

control of *Bluebell*. Luckily, she washed onto some of the rocks, but we couldn't stay there long.

The wind was building from the north, which forced us offshore. On the other side of those rocks, the lake opened up, and the storm blew unimpeded for 25 kilometers. Whitecaps crowned the steep waves, even though the fetch, or distance across open water, was only 100 or 200 meters. Conditions in the middle of the lake would be deadly. We rafted up and planned one last crossing to the mainland, where we could set up camp and hunker down.

Alie and I pulled as hard as we could to bridge the remaining 75 meters to the mainland shore. The wind shoved our bow toward the open water, and we fought our way closer to the bank a few inches at a time. When our boat finally crunched onto land, we splashed to shore and pulled our canoes onto a beautiful crescent beach below the ridge of an esker. We hiked our gear bags up the beach, away from the kitchen area, in search of flat land. The wind grew every minute.

Alie, Jen, and I worked together to set up our tent. The pegs pulled out of the ground and sprayed gravel, and wind hauled at the fabric as we fought to push the poles in. We had to yell to be heard. The boys were at work on a second tent 75 meters away. We moved our tent to a more sheltered spot, where we tried, once again, to peg it down. I thought we had it secured when a powerful gust filled the tent, yanked out all of its pegs, and sent it high into the air.

Jen hung on to one corner of the fly, just above the buckle, and ran with the tent as it sailed toward the lake. Alie and I took off after her.

Jen had less than 100 meters to slow the tent before it hit the water, but it kept accelerating. She ran like a kid with an oversized kite until the rainfly started to rip. Alie and I heard it tearing, distorting as the fabric changed shape and picked up speed. Jen tripped and landed on her chest, head facing the water, nylon sail still gripped in her right hand.

I had nearly caught up when the tent started dragging Jen through the gravel. With a final snarl, it ripped free, leaving Jen trampled on shore. I sprinted past her as the tent swooped skyward and then plummeted, partially deflated, into the lake. It stopped for a moment, until the wind found a new purchase and dragged it away.

Get the tent get the tent get the tent, I thought. *The water is cold,* I reminded myself as I closed in on the lake. Hypothermia would be better than losing the tent. *I'm still wearing my* PFD.

I ran into the water up to my chest and started swimming. I grabbed the fly at the same instant the ice water breached my clothing and struck my skin. I heaved back toward land. Jen had recovered and followed me into the water up to her thighs. She grabbed my arm; then Alie ran in and grabbed hers.

We pulled the soggy tent back into our arms.

The guys had almost finished erecting their tent when I looked up, incredulous, to realize they hadn't heard a thing. The wind's howl had drowned us out as it shredded our little home and dragged us across the beach.

"Hey!" I screamed. They came running.

I climbed into their tent to change and beat back the cold while the others set up our third shelter and reinforced them both with extra pegs and rocks at each corner, inside and out. The first tent lay soaked and broken under a third matrix of stones. The air temperature had dropped to 1 degree Celcius. We regrouped for lunch to the east of our camp in the true shelter of huge moss-covered rocks left behind by glaciers. We were doling out the chocolate when a muffled thump reached our ears.

Tim scrambled up the rise to look down at camp.

"That sounds like a boat," said Jen.

"Boat in the water!" Tim yelled. He took off toward the beach.

I sprinted behind him, losing ground. I shoved the chocolate in my hand into my pocket.

My mind scrambled for a plan, and I decided to swim after the lost canoe, even though I was wearing my only remaining dry clothes.

"Where are you going?" Tim yelled when he saw me sprinting for the water. He had already grabbed two paddles and was dragging a second boat toward the lake. Still not thinking clearly, I leapt into the boat while it was still grounded, 10 meters from shore.

"Get out!"

By now, Drew was next to us, keeping his eye on the first boat as it blew offshore with the storm. It had landed upside down, thank God, so we had a chance of catching it. Alie and Jen ran to our third boat, which was starting its own log roll. Levi tossed us an extra throw rope, and we shot away from the beach under the force of three paddlers and a hurricane-force wind. It pushed against our backs like a heavy hand.

"We're almost there!" I yelled.

Drew reached out from the bow to grab the submerged boat, but the wind sped us past it.

"Turn around! Turn around!" Drew called.

The wind threatened to force us into the open water. But if the fetch got too big and we tried to change our direction, the waves would swamp us.

Tim pried his paddle against the water and turned us. We balanced carefully and fought back upwind to our canoe, tied a throw rope to its bow, and pulled ourselves back to shore where we could haul it in safely. I flopped back against the sand to catch my breath.

We tied everything down.

Two hours later, I filled up on pasta and pesto sauce hastily prepared behind a rock by Jen and Tim, then headed to bed.

Alie, Jen, and I lay jammed together in one tent inside a circle of stones that locked down the floor; we had to raise our voices to be heard. The wind bent the tent poles. Gusts snapped the nylon fly and created a violent luffing. The fabric pulled up against my back—the tent wanted to launch skyward. Our tent sat behind the crest of an esker, partially protected, but the walls still shook out of control. A loud crack announced the next squall. Rain lashed the fly, and the wall bent inward, pressing against Alie's cheek.

I tucked in tight between my two roommates. I held out a camera and took a portrait of our faces bent together and showing teeth and wind-burnt skin. We all wore our hats and jackets at the slumber party. It was only the three of us in the world that night. Somewhere off to our left and down the hill the three men sardined into our remaining tent, but they couldn't have heard us if we had called out to them. I worried the wind would tear away the walls and ceiling to leave us lying on the tent floor, exposed to the darkening sky.

CHAPTER 9

SEARCH

None of us were in shape to travel the next morning, though the wind had calmed considerably. Drew, Alie, Jen, and Tim teamed up to reorganize the packs, clean the wannigan, and do a food inventory. Levi and I contemplated the pile of wet nylon that needed a second life. The tent itself only required minor repairs, but the fly was ripped nearly in two.

"That must have been a hurricane force wind," Levi said, "and we need to fix it up to withstand another one."

I fetched the repair kit, and we climbed into one of the other tents to mastermind the fix. We pinned the 8-foot-long Y-shaped rip with precision and began to sew. We worked toward each other with tiny stitches, as even as we could manage.

"It's like surgery," I said. We barely spoke. I focused solely on the tiny motions of my needle. Back home, I would have found the task tedious and annoying; I would have wanted to be doing something else. It took us four hours to put the pieces back together.

"Ta da!" I said when we presented our work to the others, "Can you find the seam?"

IT FELT GOOD to put the lakes and their extremes behind us, but we felt closer for having been through them. It was time to shift our focus to the white water that would only get bigger as we inched toward the ocean. Over the next four days, we stepped up our technique and confidence as the rapids grew in power and complexity. I would perch on a boulder at water level and read each twist of the waves. Which rocks were deep enough to clear, which curlers soft enough to break through. I needed to memorize the river's intentions and plan our reactions. Then I would stand with the others, often Tim and Levi, and we would confer by pointing features out to each other and speaking in code: "See that pillow behind the small curler? Not the river right one. Next to the rooster tail. We need to punch through that vee but avoid the boil." Once we agreed, we would make sure everyone knew the plan; then I would walk back to the boat while chanting it under my breath, "Vee, left of the pillow, back ferry right, nose past the hole, eddy out river right." All of the features would look different from the top of the set, so I had to find landmarks and remember the plan.

Each day the forces intensified. More and more often, the plan included a critical maneuver that took me to the edge of my comfort zone. *Whatever you do, don't touch that eddy line.* Jen was keen to learn, but the harder the rapids got, the more difficult it was to work on skill building. We just had to get through it before my heart jumped out of my chest. We would review the rapid together, and I would say something upbeat like "Okay, let's do this!"

※

LATE ON THE cold afternoon of our twenty-fifth day, we arrived at Rock Rapids—a dozen kilometers of ledges, falls, submerged rocks, and recirculating waves that we would have to portage and paddle. The river flowed swiftly: dark, loud, and as wide as a city block. As we back-paddled into camp, we noticed a pile of gear and two green canoes, too close to the rushing water, on a small island near the far shore.

Rocks blocked our view of the island, so perhaps we couldn't see the people, or maybe the pile was a food cache. I felt too cold to think. The sharp wind and near-zero temperatures had returned, which kept away the mosquitoes and blackflies, but the persistent chill made us hungry and clumsy.

That evening, the sky hung like sheet metal, overcast without visible clouds. Only three colors remained: black in the river, silver caps on the waves, and the drab olive of lichen. Nobody took pictures. The bank curved around our camp like an amphitheater; in the distance, rapids rumbled an ominous soundtrack.

A tarp broke the worst of the wind at our kitchen site, but tendrils of air still breached my filthy pants, long johns, double toque, and down-filled coat. My fingers ached as I lit the stove and fumbled through food bags to find lentils and rice. Jen and Alie lugged packs up the hill and looked for tent sites. Levi tinkered near the boats, rechecking a spray-deck repair and calibrating his barometer. Tim and Drew lashed a broken seat back together using parachute cord and a piece of wood. Their newest game was to pretend they were Jacques and Jean-Luc, Quebecois voyageurs who adored the tundra. And Drew asked questions about the wildlife, Tim's favorite subject. On the water, Drew's posture and paddle stroke had begun to loosen, and he seemed to be drawing strength from each of our successes and worrying less. Tim, in turn, took strength from Drew's renewed courage.

※

THE NEXT MORNING, the weather was blustery but clear, and there were still no bugs—perfect for portaging. The open sky restored breadth and contrast to the landscape and revealed bright patches of heather and lousewort. The river shone and chattered. We took a load of gear down a caribou trail past the first set of rapids, a journey of about twenty minutes. On the way back, I couldn't get the image of the silent camp near the far shore out of my mind.

Tim and I wanted to investigate. But Drew didn't want us to cross the river. The current sucked the water into whitecaps, and sliding backward during the crossing could send us into miles of chutes and ledges. If that happened, we wouldn't survive the first corner.

"It's too far," Drew told us. "The current's too fast."

Levi was confident we could make it. Jen and Alie didn't say anything. Our policy was never to do something if one person in the group was uncomfortable. In this case, only two of us would take the risk directly, but a bad outcome for us would affect everyone else. In general, we tried to keep things as equal as possible, but that didn't always work, and we weren't always equal. Tim and I had logged a lot of miles, and we had much more experience reading water than Drew did.

"Make your own choice," Drew said, "but I think that staying here is the smartest decision for the group and most consistent with what we agreed to."

My ego dug in. I wouldn't be dominated by Drew's fear. Part of me stuck up for him—he was committed to our safety—but his thinking was skewed by his nerves.

"We wouldn't go if it wasn't safe," I said.

We headed down to the river.

Fueled by fear and the tension with Drew, I took up my best paddling posture. Knees spread and braced against the hull. Back straight, leaning forward from the waist. My blade thrust far in front for quick strokes and maximum power. Tim would control our angle from the stern; all I had to do was paddle like hell.

I began to paddle forward, hard, while Tim nosed us into the flow. We would use a forward ferry to move the boat across the current. By pointing our bow slightly toward the opposite shore, the current would push on our exposed hull and take us there. The more we pointed across the current, the faster we would move. If we opened our hull too much, we risked being spun broadside and losing ground. If we slipped back too far, the river would feed us to its rapids.

I saw nothing but the tip of the bow and the waves off the starboard quarter. Our boat crept toward the island. River splash jostled my ears. Halfway there, my low shoulder started to burn. Sweat prickled across my sternum.

"More power!" Tim yelled over the rush.

I stared into the middle distance and dug in.

I couldn't tell from the pull of the water how much we were slipping back relative to shore. There was a place behind us where the downhill pull of the river would overpower our boat and force us to ride it out. I could feel that rapid licking our heels. The canoe surged ahead with each stroke, but it felt like we were stuck in one spot until gravel clawed our hull on the other side.

We yanked the boat out of the water and saw that we had actually gained ground in the crossing. On our way to the abandoned gear, we passed the two green canoes, which sat overturned and parallel to each other by the river's edge. Twenty paces farther on, five green canvas canoe packs slumped in a circle. Thin leather straps crisscrossed over the tops to close them, but other items lay strewn on the ground: a bag of flour, a four-liter Coleman fuel container, one boot. Off to the side, six paddles had been stacked on the rocks. A beautiful Werner with a carbon-fiber shaft caught my eye; it was probably worth two hundred bucks.

"Hello?" Tim cried. "Is anybody here?"

"Hello?" I echoed.

We split up on the small gravel island and scanned the ground. A mound of green at the island's downstream tip, only fifty paces away, rose above the rocks. Crowberry and goose droppings tangled down the back of it. No tents. The air seemed still, despite the wind, and the tundra took on the closeness of a deserted apartment.

"There's nobody here," I said, stating the obvious.

We worked the cracked straps from their buckles and peeled back the fabric. The plastic liners inside each pack were open. In the first four, blackened pots, stoves, fuel, sacks of parboiled rice, and cake mixes were jumbled together in messy piles; the rubber limbs of hip waders sprang out of the fifth. Each green flank of canvas declared "Camp Widjiwagan" and a phone number printed in faded black marker.

Tim walked back around the island to look for any other clues. It was a terrible campsite, and only inexperience or mishap could have made the campers choose it. I scanned the gravel by the packs for scraps of evidence. Upstream from us, the river widened to a kilometer across, riffling and shallow with exposed rocks at each bank. Across the river, the rocky arena of our previous night's campsite sat empty, the others having portaged all of our gear. Downstream, the river rumbled and shot froth into the air. A hike up into the hills, from the backside of the island, wouldn't have been impossible from where I stood. It was only a short hop to the mainland. Maybe the girls had used their third canoe to reach a hiking spot. *Why would they risk landing on this island in the first place? How did they get away from here?*

We didn't have paper, a pen, or a camera. We committed four digits of the camp phone number to memory and used the dials on our compasses to record the last six. We flipped the canvas closed and cinched the straps back in place before heading to the river.

✸

BACK ON THE other side, we found Drew, Alie, Jen, and Levi in the lee of a hill, lounging in the broken sunlight with the lunch bucket open and a bannock feast ready.

They waited for us before starting to eat. I felt bad about my earlier stubbornness.

We agreed to call the RCMP, and I started practicing in my head.

"My name is Jennifer Kingsley, and I am traveling with the Irvin group on the Back River in Nunavut. Our coordinates are 65° 54.906′ north, 98° 37.674′ west," I recited. "We've found an abandoned camp with a marked absence of life jackets, sleeping bags, clothes, and personal gear. We are above a long and dangerous set of rapids."

Levi dug up our satellite phone, and I dialed the RCMP in Yellowknife from the number we had printed on the front of our recipe book. The little black bars in the top left corner of the screen wouldn't come up. The battery was charged but no signal. We were getting too far north. I tried anyway and got a busy signal. I tried three times. We loaded the boats, and I tried again. As I secured our spray deck, I struggled to get my imagination under control.

Now that we had portaged the first rapid in the series, the river calmed enough for us to cross back to the other side. We would be downstream of the abandoned camp, and we wouldn't be able to get back to it without crossing a small channel, but at least we could begin a search. Farther downstream, the rapids ramped up again, but we would think about that in the morning.

It was getting late by the time we had set up camp. We decided to search for an hour and a half: Levi and I would head upstream toward the camp, Tim and Alie downstream. Each search party took a first-aid kit and extra clothes. Jen and Drew stayed put to cook lentil barley stew and kept dialing our useless satellite phone.

Before we left, I pulled Tim aside. "Are you okay?" I asked. He didn't say anything. "What if we find, you know ..."

"It's okay," he said, and we parted.

As Levi and I skirted the upstream canyon, I stared down into rapids you try not to think about. You know they are there because you've read the map and because the current beckons, and when you look from upstream, the river seems to disappear. If you stop paying attention, the slick talk of the current will lure you in. The water picked up speed to become black and glossy, like a vinyl record, then exploded into whiteness. The boiling undercurrents promised to break us or hold us under. *What will I do if I see a bright life jacket down there?*

Levi and I climbed the banks in silence until we could see unexplored ponds and streams, Lower MacDougall Lake, and the girls' abandoned camp in the distance. Turnaround time. Nothing to report.

When I finally took my eyes away from the horizon to look down at the hillside below us, I slowly reached for Levi's arm. He looked at me, then followed my eyes. Four wolves were climbing straight toward us, padding easily over angled boulders.

We stood still at first, mesmerized by the casual rhythm of their gait. Their legs chose each rock blindly yet never missed. Yellow-white twists of fur lifted and dropped with each step; their eyes fixed me in place. They climbed straight for us and showed no sign of stopping until two broke off to our right. *Are they flanking us?* Levi and I shrank back on our haunches behind a boulder, I unholstered my bear spray—just in case—and we waited for the wolves to crest the rise. After a few moments, Levi and I stood up again, but the wolves had vanished. I scrutinized each rock with my binoculars, picking out lichen and cotton grass, but we never saw those wolves again.

Our own camp came back into sight as we headed downstream. We had twenty minutes left on our time limit, but the other searchers were back early. We hustled down the rocks, back to our friends. Tim and Alie stood by our camp kitchen with Jen and Drew. The four of them formed a circle and stared down into the middle of it. A damp patch of sand bled out around their shoes. In the center sat a large, soggy backpack, just like the ones at the camp. Levi and I stepped into the circle, but nobody spoke. The pack's canvas bulged toward me. Clipped to the outside was a small beige teddy bear.

CHAPTER 10

FORWARD

Alie slid the straps from the pack and folded back the top flaps. She dug in and began lifting out dripping objects: running shoes, a sleeping bag, a bloated paperback, a wallet, a half-finished knitting project, and a river stone. The stack of clothes was all cotton, which sucks heat from your body in a flash. Then Alie found a journal, still dry in its plastic bag. My stomach flipped when she opened the cover to reveal loopy blue handwriting.

"Her name is Rosemary,"[1] Alie said. "Her last entry is from July 14."

"Six days ago," said Levi.

Alie flipped through the pages and read a few sections, little tidbits about the journey. Enough for us to see Rosemary was having fun.

"They left that book at Buliard's cabin on July 10, and we found it on July 12," said Drew. "There is no way they could have made it here by July 14. I guess she wasn't keeping up with her journal." So we didn't know how many days ago the bag had been lost.

We put the pack back together and got camp ready for the night. The ledges and hilly rock piles that created the rapids up- and downstream also surrounded our camp. Levi suggested we hike our red canoe to the top of a nearby hill.

"If they are still out here, let's help them find us," he said.

Tim helped portage the boat to the peak a few hundred meters away. The Back River basin is pretty flat, so even a 50-meter hill sticks up like a flagpole. They flipped the canoe at the summit and lashed it to the rocks.

I approached Drew as he stowed the satellite phone.

"No luck?" I asked, though I knew the answer.

"It's weird," he said. "It worked for me not too long ago."

I didn't understand. We had agreed not to use the phone.

"I know. But I used it to call Hilary." His wife. "I miss her."

"But we said—"

"I know. But it worked last week."

Safe inside my tent that night, my mind raced. I imagined Rosemary dragging herself toward our temporary beacon. Based on her backpack, the landscape that she imagined— and that her summer camp imagined—was different from this one. We had not been expecting the same things, she and I, when she shoved fistfuls of underwear and jogging pants into her bag.

When we first found out about the girls back in Yellowknife, we'd heard that they wouldn't be paddling any white water, yet they chose a route with dozens of sets of rapids. The camp hadn't equipped them with spray decks, which are essential for keeping water out of the boat in big weather and waves. Perhaps they didn't want to tempt the girls by giving them that equipment, but it meant riskier lake crossings and heavy-weather paddling. None of it mattered anymore. We just wanted to know where they were.

✳

MORNING BROUGHT SHIT cubed weather, so Drew and Levi made pancakes. We all felt tired and worried. We wouldn't travel until the weather settled.

The men decided to hike down to Sinclair Falls that day. The falls marked the end of the deadly rapids, and they wanted to stretch their legs and take a look. It would be 20 kilometers, round trip. Alie, Jen, and I would take the day to sleep and catch up on writing our journals. It was the third day of wondering about those girls, but there was nothing we could do without a connection to the outside world.

I watched the men walk away across the tundra and let the wind settle into my ears. The sky had grown heavy overnight, leaching the color away again. I imagined what we looked like from above. I could see the tents like heads of pins and the colorful specks of Tim, Drew, and Levi walking away. There were caribou out there somewhere, and bears and wolves that followed them. I could barely see myself from above. I had come north to rediscover the feeling of being small, but in the midst of an unexpected mystery, I didn't like it.

I picked a sprig of yellow cinquefoil to remind myself of the tundra's brightness. Back in the tent, I crawled into my sleeping bag with my clothes on and crushed the flower into my journal. "I know I have to get over it," I wrote, "but I can't believe how fucking cold it is—all the time. We sleep, eat, wait. I hope the girls had a phone that worked."

✳

DREW'S "YOO-HOOOO!" BLEW into camp around suppertime. He marched toward us with another pack on his back.

"We found it in an eddy," Tim said.

The pack looked like the ones from the island: same writing in black marker, same leather straps to close it. Drew opened the lid to reveal food stores, different from ours. He laid out potato flakes, cocoa, rice, butterscotch chips, and just-add-water cheesecake on the ground. And they had onions; we hadn't brought any fresh vegetables. My mouth watered. Drew then reached down the side of the pack and unearthed a hard, black waterproof case. Their satellite phone.

"What the hell?" said Tim.

"Oh, no," Alie followed.

We all had the same run of questions in our minds. If we had their phone, how could they get out? Many groups traveled with only one piece of communication equipment. Were they were still out there somewhere? Where? The rapids themselves could have been fatal, and if they survived those, exposure would be the next threat. If they had been separated, some would have to survive without the food, clothing, and shelter they had lost to the river.

Although the phone deepened our worry, it could also solve our problem. I unsnapped the lid and slid the phone from its foam nest. I saw with relief that it was an Iridium phone, not a GlobalStar like ours. Iridium had a more extensive constellation of satellites and provided service all the way to the poles. I pushed the power button and watched with relief as the service bars came up.

I dialed the RCMP in Yellowknife and managed to say, "Hello?" before we got cut off. It took a few more tries before I got out the lines I had been practicing.

"My name is Jennifer Kingsley, and I am traveling with the Irvin group on the Back River in Nunavut. We came upon an abandoned campsite yesterday, and we want to know if you have any information about a group from Camp Widjiwagan."

"Just a minute, please," the dispatcher answered.

A moment later: "Jack Kruger here, Yellowknife Search and Rescue."

I explained our situation—the camp, the search, the abandoned satellite phone—but Kruger hadn't heard of the girls.

"Call me back at 1900," he said. He would check with some of the detachments in Nunavut. Still, wouldn't he know if there had been a recent rescue?

Jen made supper with one of the girls' onions—our first fresh vegetable in weeks. My mouth filled with saliva even as a lump swelled in my throat. It felt wrong to use their food before we knew if they were alive or dead. I wanted to know whom we were stealing from. Nausea rose from my gut, and I forced it down with reason. *They don't need it, no matter what happened.*

Jen caught me staring at her. "We don't want to waste it."

At 1900, I dialed Officer Kruger again.

"Quickly, before I lose you," he said when the connection finally held. "I talked to the RCMP in Baker Lake, and the campers are all there. They were evacuated on Monday." The day before we had seen the camp.

The line started to crackle. *The girls must have had a satellite beacon like ours.* No time to ask questions, and I couldn't afford to run the battery down.

"Thank you," I said.

"Enjoy your trip," Kruger replied before he cut us off from the rest of the world.

"Well," Alie said into the silence after I hung up the phone. "That's good, right?"

Good, but strange. A disappearing act. An example of how technology can drop us into the wild and quickly pluck us out again. The girls had gone, and we were caught in their wake.

From what we had seen, I didn't think the girls were prepared for that river. At the same time, I had dumped a canoe myself on a much easier stretch of water. Sometimes it's only a hair's breadth between bad judgment and bad luck.

We decided to use the camp phone to call Drew's dad, Greg Gulyas, whom we had appointed as our main safety contact. Now that we had a working phone, it made sense to keep it, and we feared the camp would cancel the service if they thought it was lost on the tundra.

"If we call Greg, I don't want him to contact the other families," I said. "No news is good news."

Since I had found out about Drew's clandestine phone call and spoken to Kruger "on the outside," I was obsessed with protecting our wilderness quarantine. We wanted to get away from everyone and everything familiar—that was what we had agreed. It was time to defend that agreement.

"If he starts calling everyone, they'll worry. They won't be able to help themselves." I wanted my fifty-day communication break. That was the plan. "It's simpler this way, no?"

No one put up much of an argument; everyone was probably too tired to care.

Drew slid the phone from its case again and dialed his parents.

"Remember," I nagged, "we need to conserve the battery for emergencies."

"Dad-it's-Drew-it's-not-an-emergency-our-group-is-all-okay," he announced in one breath.

He explained the situation concisely and asked that Greg call the camp to request permission to use the phone until the end of August. "Gotta go, Dad. We're fine. Gotta go. Love you too."

We clicked back into the sounds of the river and each other. The outside world had been pushed back into its corner, for the moment at least.

WE DIDN'T WANT any other paddlers to worry as we had—though there weren't likely to be any until the following year—so Drew, Jen, and Levi left the next morning for the girls' camp. They would try to wade back to the island and leave notes with the remaining gear. Hopefully, they would come back with some of the girls' awesome paddles, too. Alie prepared six waterproof notes to stash with the abandoned packs.

"The owners of this gear were evacuated safely on July 18, 2005. Take any gear that might be of use to you, but please leave this note with the remaining packs."

It took Drew, Jen, and Levi two hours to hike up and attempt to reach the camp. Drew and Levi donned wet suits to wade across a narrow channel, and Jen belayed them from shore with a throw rope, but the current was too much. They built a cairn for the notes instead, took some pictures, and hiked back to us.

After lunch, we left the dreary campsite we had been in for three nights. We took Rosemary's bag and the food bag to the first portage, where we planned to stash them.

"Now that the Dead Girls aren't dead, can we take their stuff?" Jen asked.

"The Dead Girls?" said Levi.

"Seems fitting."

"Morbid."

Alie went back through the bag for Rosemary's wallet, journal, and knitting. We figured she would want those things. We also kept the river stone she had collected.

"Who wants what?" Alie asked about the remaining pile of junk. She took Rosemary's yoga pants and running shoes, and I scored her charcoal gray cashmere sweater. It was a couple of sizes too small, but I could fit it over my grubby undershirt.

Meanwhile, Jen and Tim dug through the food pack for anything we would eat; we couldn't carry it all. Onions, rice, butterscotch chips, and cheesecake filling made the cut. We added more notes to the packs and stowed them out of sight of the river.

"Let's get out of here," said Tim.

We picked our way through the sets of rapids that afternoon and finally gained some distance on the Dead Girls—the nickname had stuck—but it wasn't long before another bright throw bag and backpack caught our attention.

This was starting to feel like a chore.

"This one is Katherine,"[2] Alie said once she'd found the diary. Half of it was still dry.

Katherine had packed three paperbacks, five bandanas, endless underwear, a bag of craft supplies, and a stack of cotton clothing similar to Rosemary's. Everything bulged, swollen with river water, from her overstuffed "waterproof" bags.

"Let's take the wallet and journal with us," Alie said. "And maybe this homemade hat and address book. What would you do with an address book out here?"

Then we descended on the bag like a bunch of pickpockets. Tundra Shopping, Part 3.

Jen helped herself to some fleecy socks, and I took tiny fleece tights, which I later sewed into a neck tube and some wrist warmers. Another note, another stash job, and we were gone. It's amazing what can become routine.

✴

I SPENT FIVE years wondering what it had been like for the Widjiwagan girls to be in that wilderness. I felt sure they must have been terrified, despite the happy ending. (Happy, or simply not disastrous?) I imagined a hundred versions of what had happened before the helicopter whisked them away.

The story made a small sensation in the canoeing community later that year when a paddling magazine published an article criticizing the girls' rescue. The evacuation would have been funded by public money, and rescues often cost somewhere in the ballpark of $100,000. The writer, Bill Layman, who had published on this subject before, rightly pointed out that paddlers must use the correct technology, which is a Personal Locator Beacon, or PLB, specifically engineered for recreational use. Some canoeists, especially at that time, were guilty of using systems designed either for ships (Emergency Position Indicating Radio Beacons, or EPIRBS) or planes (Emergency Locator Transmitters, or ELTS), leading to inappropriate rescue measures and even extra costs.

Layman also argued that some people ("dumb paddlers") should "learn to bowl"[3] instead of canoeing, and he put the girls from Camp Widjiwagan in that category. Using bad secondhand information, he suggested the girls could have self-rescued with their remaining canoes and avoided the cost of calling for help. Layman's inaccurate reporting "does everyone a disservice,"[4] as Tim was quick to point out in a letter to the editor; however, Layman did raise an important issue. Because satellite technology makes it easier to call for help, it may entice people into situations they are not ready for or tempt them to call for help they don't really need. But evaluating who is in what category is next to impossible. There are no clean lines between inexperience, accident, and emergency. And the question of who should pay for which rescues—the government, as an extension of emergency services, or the "client," if it's not a proper emergency—is just as complicated. Some people, like Layman, boast about their own safety record as if success were simply a matter of preparedness—but accidents *do* happen, even to experienced trippers. We can reduce our risk, but there are no guarantees. There never will be.

In 2007, Alie published a story in a Canadian magazine; in it, she mentioned the girls' ordeal. Two of the campers responded to the article online. "The Author of the Diary You Discovered" thanked us for returning her journal—no one had told her that it had come from us—and she invited us to contact her. The message ended with "I'd love to hear more!" The second response, from Terri, was less friendly. She simply said she would like to discuss the "actual" experience.5 What had the "actual" experience become by then?

In early 2010, I called the RCMP in Baker Lake and made a formal request about the events of 2005, but I didn't get any information. I talked to Jack Kruger, but he barely remembered the incident, since it hadn't occurred in his district. I used the names I could decipher from *The Man Who Mapped the Arctic* to track the girls down on Facebook and then email. After reading their replies to Alie's article, I didn't think talking to them would be a problem—but I got only one positive response, and right away something changed. She was going to call me but then emailed to say she didn't want to talk anymore. There were aspects of the trip she was not willing to speak about. "Please don't use my name," she wrote. No one would answer my messages after that.

Was there a flurry of emails as they consulted each other? What could be so hard to speak about after five years? I imagined a lingering terror or profound embarrassment. I wondered how such an intense event affected their relationships with each other. Amidst weeks of isolation, experiences on the land become heavy with meaning. What takes only moments to happen can linger for a lifetime. I imagined bug-bitten girls, some dripping wet, waiting for the helicopter's whir. And then a message came in. One of them was willing to talk.

I pressed the phone to my ear and held my breath as she recounted the story I had waited so long to hear. "It was the end of a tiring day," she began.

The set of rapids loomed, and they didn't want to shoot it: too cold, too tired. The group began to ferry to shore—

one canoe at a time until they reached the island where we later found their things. The leader (just one) and the last two girls (one sitting in the middle as we had suspected) attempted their forward ferry. They faced upstream, digging their blades into the waves as their boat slipped backward. The leader shouted encouragement as the river overcame them. I know that moment well, the certainty in your gut that you have lost the arm wrestle. They spun to face their opponent, to try and beat it at its game. But the fear, instability, fatigue, and lack of position were too much. The boat tipped. "They went all the way down."

The remaining four ran to the end of the island, but their friends had disappeared. They scanned the water, waiting. The minutes stretched out. Did they hold hands? Pray?

"Finally, we saw little black figures walking." Three young women, soaking wet and stripped of all of their gear, climbed back into view on the far side of the river.

Now a gulf, too frightening to cross, severed them from each other. They doubted their strength to overcome it. One boat, three bags, and the satellite phone were gone. The survivors paced up and down on the other side, shouting over the river-roar. The girls yelled to each other until the dry ones headed for the highest point. They had one remaining piece of communications equipment, a satellite beacon, and it was time to follow the instructions: *Remove cover. Push button.* They paced and kept watch. They took turns lying down and jogging for warmth. After six hours, the helicopter.

Reunited at an apartment in Baker Lake, they swapped tales of the near-tragedy. Who cried, who called out for her mother. But, at least for the woman I spoke with, relief that they were safe vied with heavy disappointment that they hadn't finished the trip as planned.

At Camp Widjiwagan, the voyageur groups from previous years show slides of their Arctic trips; it's part of the tradition to get new voyageurs ready: "You feel impressed," she said. Of the North: "I loved being in that landscape." But after the accident, the girls wanted to reassure themselves of their skills, their love for the place—before they grew afraid of it.

I am torn between an understanding of this woman's story and a suspicion of it. Perhaps they were too tired and cold to run that rapid, but did they know it was too difficult to run under any circumstance? If they were experienced enough to run that river, why didn't they equip themselves with spray decks, which I considered essential for safety on the Back? She was seventeen, "only seventeen," one might say, but she quickly reminded me that "seventeen- and eighteen-year-olds are pretty able-bodied. They can do a lot. And you can't guarantee safety." She sounded confident about her training and the structure of her camp, but wondered if that trip would be better for people who are more mature. On the other hand, "It's one of the most meaningful things I've ever done. My resilience and independence come from that trip in particular." The young woman's name was Jenny; she reminded me of myself, and I can't reconcile her confidence with the mess of unprotected boats and craft supplies we found.

I have also taken trips I was less than one hundred percent prepared for; that's how I learned. The next time I plan something big, I won't be one hundred percent prepared for that either. And many people have discouraged me from doing the things I love most, but their fear—not only of the wilderness but also that I won't ever have a "normal" life— is a reflection of my own, and I've learned not to give it too much weight.

After a few days in Baker Lake, the young women gathered some new gear and flew back to the tundra. They couldn't go to the Back again, but they flew west of Baker Lake and then paddled back, to "bring it home," as the staff at Widjiwagan put it.

Jenny said it wasn't the same, but it was something.

WE STOWED OUR shopping spree finds in our packs and continued downstream. By then, the final obstacle in this series of rapids we'd been hung up in for four days was within striking distance: Sinclair Falls. The approach emphasized how far we'd come since the Baillie River, almost a month ago. The falls dropped in a series of ledges followed by gigantic waves. Even the cleanest lines—the paths through the rapids one could attempt with open boats—were three times too big for our canoes. The only routes we could consider snuck around the fringes.

With the girls' ordeal behind us and the temperature rising, our mood lightened. We found a small route on river right, a "hammy hamster" we called it, where we could line up the boats and crash into rocks without any consequences. Tossing consequences aside for a few hours was good medicine. When Tim and Alie's boat got stuck, Levi, Jen, and I stood up on a ledge and mooned them. Then Levi pointed Jen and me through a "clear" channel, only to laugh his head off when we smashed into a rock and stopped dead.

Levi stands by one of many rapids. CREDIT: TIM IRVIN

By evening, we'd made the bottom of the falls and set up camp. Alie and I cooked a feast of squash soup with dumplings, gado gado (pasta and peanut sauce), and a no-bake cheesecake with a bannock crust, courtesy of Widjiwagan. We didn't even talk about the girls that night. We just sat around eating their food and wearing their clothes.

CHAPTER 11

RELEASE

The boat George Back used to get down and back up the Thlew-ee-choh was literally his lifeboat. Thirty feet long and double-pointed, it was equipped with oars, poles, and a simple rig for sailing. It also had ample room for storage and carried over 1,500 kilograms (3,300 pounds) of cargo, plus ten men, a few dogs, and extra oars and rigging. Carpenters had built it from knotty wood harvested a short distance from Fort Reliance, and it was impressively sturdy, but not strong enough to be dragged along a portage. With steel runners fitted to the bottom, it could be skated over ice (with a great deal of exertion), but for dodging rapids, the boat had to be carried. No one told Back until the last minute about this hernia-inducing task; the entire crew together could barely manage it when the boat was dry, let alone soaked with river water. The men carried pitch and tar to help with repairs. If anything happened to that boat, they were finished.

On April 25, 1834, before the spring thaw had begun in earnest, there had been a knock on the door at Fort Reliance. A messenger bearing a letter burst into the room and

announced, "He is returned, sir! . . . Captain Ross, sir—
Captain Ross is returned."[1] The men in the Ross party had
been missing for four years, and the primary purpose of
Back's expedition was to search for them. The previous fall,
after surviving on stores left at the Arctic coast by explorer
William Parry, Ross and his men had managed to flag
down a whaling ship and hitch a ride to England. When
they arrived home, in October, they sent a letter to Back
with the news of their safe arrival, but the news took six
months to reach him. Back's expedition changed once he
knew the Ross party was safe. The descent of the new river
became purely exploratory; Back would attempt to reach
the ocean and map a new section of coastline. He decided
to cut his travel party from two boats to one, since he no
longer needed room for the rescued men—and by diminish-
ing the crew, he could speed his progress and stretch his
severely depleted food supply.

He made the announcement in May, as the first patches
of green began to show through the snow. Soon geese
would fly overhead and willow catkins would emerge. On
June 7, Captain Back, Dr. King, and their crew left Fort
Reliance. Back had sent his trusty fixer, McLeod, ahead to
cache meat for them, and he hired extra porters to carry
the pemmican, flour, cocoa, rum, and macaroni they would
need for three months.

"There is something exciting in the first start even upon an
ordinary journey," Back wrote. "The bustle of preparation—
the act of departing, which seems like a decided step
taken—the prospect of change, and consequent stretching
out of the imagination—have at all times the effect of stir-
ring the blood, and giving a quicker motion to the spirits."[2]

The men's first task was to climb out of the watershed to the height of land and find the headwaters of the Thlew-ee-choh again. In the relatively flat country of the eastern mainland Arctic, the maze of lakes and small streams makes it difficult to find a clear route from one drainage into another. Strangely, Back left his notes from the previous year behind, which didn't make things any easier, and the ice-filled spring landscape confused him further. While his men spent the days hauling gear over the ice and enduring either snowstorms or buggy heat, Back spent the evenings climbing various hills to jog his memory. McLeod paralleled their track, some distance ahead, with his land-based party. His men hunted and cached meat for Back along the route and marked it with rock cairns and notes attached to tree branches. Although neither leader had much sense of the country he traveled in, this system worked somehow. Back found at least as many caches as he missed, sometimes indicated only by a tiny note flapping in the wind. Back reached the headwaters of the Thlew-ee-choh, via the north end of Aylmer Lake, on June 28, 1834.

From there, a journey into unknown regions began. The men left Dene territory and moved deeper into Inuit land, where the river had different names, including Haningayok and Ukkuhikhalik. They didn't know what lay ahead or how much the men's skill—especially that of the principal bowman, George Sinclair, and the steersman, James McKay—would be tested.

It's the details in Back's journal that surprised me most. The further I got into the minutiae of his daily travel, the more I recognized our own journey. Back's team was surprised to find so much ice and had to devise ways to cross it; they even chopped a trail with axes. His men were vexed by the alternating heat and frequent cold storms; they had chosen an unusually cold season, as we had. The men traveled nights to avoid weather, and Back even boasted about traveling light: "Only a very limited wardrobe can be allowed."[3] Back saw caribou and marveled at the goose molt; he found so many dropped feathers that "carts might have been laden with them."[4] He wrote about the hummocks on the tundra—raised humps of grass a foot wide—that look dry and inviting to the hiker, but unless you tread on them dead center (a difficult calculation) they'll twist your ankle and send you sprawling to the ground.

But we had maps, whereas Back was creating the first paper map of the area as he went. We had waterproof breathables (a "space-age fabric," as Levi liked to say) and a more reliable and varied diet. Back's convoluted description of hunger warrants a chuckle: "certain internal gnawings began to intimate the propriety of supplying the organs of digestion with some occupation which might keep them from quarrelling among themselves."[5]

I could relate to Back as a stranger to the country and someone who could not survive without extensive provisions. Although he and I come from different times, we agree on at least one thing: that "squeamishness is little heeded in such traveling as this, and shirking is quite out of the question."[6]

Back had traveled several hundred kilometers before he reached the junction with the Baillie, where our paths intersected. His descriptions of the water are lively to say the least, and he has been criticized for exaggerating its power. He devotes long paragraphs to Rock Rapids, for example, where our group found the abandoned camp. Back describes a river that "foamed, and boiled, and rushed with impetuous and deadly fury."[7] He writes about rocks 800 feet high, which I certainly never saw, but he does drive home the point that death awaits careless paddlers there.

Portaging those rapids was impossible with Back's heavy boat, so his crew emptied the cargo and tracked the boat downstream with two ropes at either end, his men poling from on-board and rock hopping from out-board. "Repeatedly did the strength of the current hurl the boat within an inch of destruction,"[8] but McKay and Sinclair kept their cool and impressed their boss. They were awarded a cup of grog to celebrate, and when they reached the falls the next day, Back named them after Sinclair.

WE HAD BARELY pulled away from Sinclair Falls when a flash of silver winked between the ripples up ahead. A strange object lolled at water level close to shore, and as we approached the silver turned to red. We all recognized it at the same time: Camp Widjiwagan Canoe #3. The final piece of the puzzle.

"This is getting weird," said Drew.

Tim and I paddled *Delilah* that day, the red 16-foot Esquif Prospecteur made with Royalex that Jen had purchased for the trip. As we came alongside the lost boat, also red, we noticed that it too was a 16-footer, which is not unusual. We landed our boats and surrounded the overturned one. When we pulled up on the gunwales, the river tugged back until we tilted the canoe slightly, broke the seal, and flipped it over in a rush of water. Only then could we see the entire hull and its labels: Esquif Prospecteur made with Royalex. Somehow, in perfect condition. From where the girls fell out of it, the boat had traveled the most treacherous 12 kilometers of the river, ending with a drop over the falls. Waterlogged maps and cameras dangled from the thwarts. A Nalgene water bottle, with drinking water sealed in, slumped against the side of the hull along with two small "dry" bags, turgid with water, and floating cameras. A small black Pelican case boasted a bone-dry SLR, a sweet-looking Nikon camera. It took film, so we couldn't cruise its memory card to peek into the past.

We started disassembling the boat immediately. Levi and Tim pulled out Leathermans to strip off the center thwart, in case we needed one, and the bow seat, to replace our broken one. We left the soggy cameras but took the Nikon to return to sender. After our salvage work was done, I snapped a picture of everyone grinning and leaning on each other and the boat, as if it were a hot rod, and it kind of was. The boat gave us pleasure. We surrounded it like bounty hunters; we couldn't step away, and that's when the impulse came.

"Let's take it," I blurted out.

Perhaps we could get a new boat out of all this craziness. It made no sense to add another canoe to our outfit, but to my delight, everyone agreed.

"Let's call her *Desiree*," said Jen, "*Delilah*'s evil twin."

"Let's ghost-ride her down Escape Rapids," Tim replied.

"Maybe we could get her home somehow?"

The scavenger's impulse burned in all of us. She was too good to leave behind. We could tow her, perhaps as far as the ocean, still hundreds of kilometers away.

I couldn't resist the image of our boat towing its empty twin, the vessel of another journey, so I tied her to our stern with a simple bowline knot, and we took off: *Delilah* and *Desiree*.

Even in the brisk current, the other boats sped ahead. *Desiree* strained at her halter; she pulled back and then sped up beside us on a rebound from the stretched line. She swerved and pulled our stern off course. I dug my paddle in and snarled, my determination fixed. We had tied ourselves to those girls, and I wasn't ready to let go.

After ten minutes of towing, Jen perked up in her seat, "Listen!"

She peered at the far bank, and we followed her gaze to find four blond wolves standing out against the horizon. One tipped its nose up and howled into the sky.

Jen laid her paddle across the gunwales, and looking to us for silent approval, cupped her mouth, threw her head back, and howled in return. The wolves froze for a moment and then trotted straight toward us.

As we tugged that boat downstream, the wolves galloped along the riverbank, yowling and skipping along. The wind whipped their fur upward as they stared at us. They looked down on our boats and chatted to each other; they made sounds I'd never heard before: trills, stable single notes, and low ruffs. Levi and I found each other's eyes. Perhaps they were the same wolves we'd seen on the hill. The four of them skipped in a line next to the six of us before they turned and blended back into the tundra.

Desiree didn't settle down. She kept dragging on us like the girls had. The shadow boat tugged like an anchor, tucked behind us like an alter ego. I J-stroked in the stern again and again to pull her back under control.

After two hours, we stopped for lunch, and I accepted that it was time to let *Desiree* go. We couldn't carry that failed journey anymore. We laughed to each other about the idea of taking her with us: "It was fun while it lasted." I didn't want to admit how much I had wanted her.

Levi and I escorted her over a rise in the bank where she wouldn't be visible from the river. We left her right-side up and filled her belly with rocks. I extracted a Sharpie marker from my life jacket pocket and wrote, "*Abandoned July 23, 2005. Paddlers safely evacuated. Feel free to take spare parts.*" Not that there were many left.

I wondered who would find her next, if anyone. It's an ill-fitting life for a canoe—full of stone, bleaching part of the year, and freezing the rest. The plastic would last a long time.

Before we left, I turned to face the boat and framed her in my vision. *Goodbye.*

✳

THE CURRENT CARRIED us on, and the sun grew stronger until we actually felt warm. The change in weather reminded me of a Hollywood movie; good things, like the conclusion of a trying experience, bring good weather. My arms relaxed in relief.

"Check it out," Tim called from the bow of our boat. "I took off my jacket and my toque at the same time! And I spy a really big star!" He pointed up to the sun.

Tim continued in his usual bow-paddler style, a mix of paddle strokes and sporadic wildlife scanning. On most days, he had to stern-paddle, which takes more focus, so when he got a day in the bow, he preferred looking around to keeping his paddle in the water. When he picked up his binoculars for the six millionth time that day, I didn't think anything of it until he stopped scanning and stared in one spot. He held his gaze steady, lowered the binos, then looked again.

Without a word, he took the binoculars off with his left hand, leaned back across the spray deck, and stretched his arm toward me. I rocked onto my knees and reached out in time to catch them in my palm.

I scanned the distance and found a couple of caribou sauntering along. We'd seen that lots of times already. I shot Tim a questioning glance, but he nodded his head in their direction again. A second look revealed not two but twenty-five or fifty animals.

I grinned and passed the binos forward again. Tim almost always found the wildlife first. We called out to the others and were heading toward them when Tim cracked a huge grin.

"Yes," he said. "Yes!"

He swung the glasses back to me a second time, and I discovered that those fifty animals had multiplied into three hundred. And they were headed our way. We took turns studying them at eight times magnification.

The caribou kept up a trot—neither relaxed nor hurried—the young, males, and females jumbled together into a giant pincushion of antlers and ears.

My heart tightened in excitement, relief, and anxiety. *We found them! But which way are they going?*

As soon as the caribou came over the horizon, on our right and still a long way off, they turned to parallel the river, targeting a peninsula in front of us. We paddled hard to gain on them, until their goal became clear: the river itself.

The leaders reached the peninsula, where the water narrowed, and they waded into the quickening current. As the caribou changed their trajectory again to cross the river, the sun lined up behind them, and each one, in turn, transformed from scruffy and brown to crisp and silhouetted. The leaders sank into the river until only their heads and a strip of their backs broke the surface. I imagined their hooves pedaling against the current—caribou on bikes. Individuals of all sizes crowded into the water, while we sat 400 meters away and stared. The black, throbbing line of antlers spiked up like lichen until the animals climbed dripping from the far side, in formation, and disappeared over the crest of the bank. We never heard a sound.

AFTER A SUPPER of veggie shepherd's pie, we gathered under the bug tent in our long underwear, jackets, and neck warmers. We chatted about the caribou and wondered if we were close to a bigger herd and if we would see them again. I prayed that we would; Tim and I had been farther back than the others during the crossing, and I felt I'd missed out a little. Jen passed around Alie's mug full of hot chocolate spiked with Kahlua from our tiny alcohol stash, and we admired the two fresh pans of fluffy cinnamon raisin buns covered in icing (with a few mosquitoes struggling in it) that we would eat for dessert. We waited for Levi, who was dressing up in a special holiday outfit. Our trip Christmas should have been on Day 25, but it had been postponed by cold temperatures and the Dead Girls

Debacle. We had rescheduled for that night to receive gifts from our Secret Santas.

Levi trotted up to the mesh and performed the bug tent swoop we had all perfected to get inside: grab the bottom of the net, lift and duck simultaneously, shift from one foot to the other, and push the mesh back to the ground with minimum bug leakage.

"Merry Christmas, everyone," Levi smiled. He sported his navy and green plaid wool shirt, an army-green wool pullover vest, and a necktie made from a strip of red webbing he'd found in our repair kit.

"Okay," said Jen, who was the most excited for the festivities, "who got Tim?" And the gift giving began.

I awarded Tim a circular orange ripstop nylon badge embroidered with navy blue flowers that I had made from repair kit materials. I called it the George Back Stop and Smell the Flowers Award for excellence in natural history observation. Tim had found a lucky Arctic hare foot, only slightly gory, which he gave to Jen, along with a poem. Jen had embroidered "Darth Vegan" on a fresh red bandana, and gave it to Levi, who performed an inaugural blow into the only clean cotton for miles. Levi's gift for Drew wasn't quite like the others, but no one expected that it would be: a handmade backstage pass to a Rod Stewart concert, complete with a personal gift pack that contained extra-strength Gold Bond body powder, a condom, and a personalized note: "Drew, Looking forward to seeing you after the show, Rod." It hadn't occurred to me that someone would bring condoms—I doubted they were just for this gag, but if anyone was hooking up I didn't know about it. Drew gave Alie a rental of his futon-sized Therm-a-Rest, along with one of his poems, and then it was my turn. Alie stood up and called on her backup singers (everyone else). They swooped out of the tent and stood in formation with Alie at the front. She pulled out a piece of paper and started in on "California Dreamin'," rewritten for me.

All our boats are long
And our packs are fat
Well, we've got a funky bug net
And the IBM *hat . . .*

They sang, danced, and stopped only occasionally to hack up a mosquito or wipe one from their eyes. At the end of the show, Alie gave me a hug, and then, in the long tradition of small gestures that mean so much more when you are far away from home, she presented me with a small Ziploc bag. Inside was a handful of valuables: jujubes, sour keys, and licorice. Where had those treats come from?

"They are from my share of the gorp. I've been saving them for you," she said. "Merry Christmas."

CHAPTER 12

REPRIEVE

oxing Day started beautifully: 12 degrees Celcius, warm muffins, and some time to lounge. I even took off a layer. When a sudden wind drop-kicked the temperature and slanting rain dripped down our necks, Drew simply said, "It was good while it lasted."

We took to the river anyway.

It wasn't long before we spotted more movement on the bank, as if the bank itself were moving. Caribou. Our journey was about to fold into theirs.

We parked the boats and wandered up to take a look. I lifted my binoculars to scan the patch of snorting animals, but there was no edge. The hundreds had grown. We settled in to watch.

The herd rippled in a mixture of action and rest. As many as half of the animals would graze or pause, though they rarely lay down, and the others wandered—aimlessly, it seemed. Just as the group appeared totally scattered, with no nucleus and no direction, one—somewhere—would startle and snap a wave of movement through the others. Large groups rushed together, like a flock of birds that swoop in synchrony across the sky, mindless of what sparked the chain reaction. When they fled, the hill darkened with bodies straining past each other until they forgot their fear and spread out again.

Sometimes a few leaders would begin walking and tug the others along by some invisible leash; yet the herd didn't seem to go anywhere. That entire mob—mothers, babies, huge bucks, and aging grannies—had to make the tree line by winter. The scars of their nose-to-tail migration score the tundra's entire face. We had followed the tiny trails ourselves many times. Watching them bob and weave across the hill with no discernible direction, I couldn't imagine they would make it very far, but if I left one group to watch another, sometimes a whole hillside would be empty by the time I looked back at it.

✳

ALIE AND I were on kitchen duty the night after that long caribou-filled day. After supper, she dumped out the last slick of dishwater and we headed back to our tent. We were sharing The Boss that night. It was late, but not dark, so we saw the packages addressed to each of us right away when we opened the vestibule. The mailman was nowhere in sight.

Alie scooped up the envelopes, and we dove into the tent's dim light. The Boss's atmosphere was sometimes rosy, sometimes a sickly beige, depending on the sun and your mood.

I stripped off my down jacket and shoved it under my chest as I sprawled onto my Therm-a-Rest. I tugged off my toque, and Alie handed me my envelope. I saw my mother's handwriting, and tears welled up. I kept quiet at first—I didn't want to interrupt Alie's excitement—and I slit the envelope to search its contents. Then I couldn't stop myself. Hot sobs erupted from my chest and tears splashed onto my bed.

"What happened, sweetie?" Alie looked surprised. "What happened?"

I couldn't answer.

Alie rolled toward me for a hug.

"I was hoping for something from home," I said.

That didn't make sense, because the letter was from home, sort of; I had a fistful of letters from Ottawa, where I had family and a few friends, but there was nothing from Victoria, where I lived. My heart dropped when I didn't see a letter from Dalton. The pain of it shocked me, and to my embarrassment, I couldn't slow my tears. I had promised nothing; yet out there I wanted everything.

Our tradition of mail had begun on the Hood River three years before. My paddling partner on that trip, Steve, had the brilliant idea of gathering letters from everyone's friends and family and secretly delivering them about half-way through the forty-six-day trip. None of us knew a thing about it, and the surprise delivery brought joy across the board. On the Back River, Levi wanted to continue the tradition. He had mentioned it once, so I wasn't entirely surprised, but I felt disappointed. Steve had been thorough; Levi had not. It was a beautiful idea, but without correspondence from anyone in Victoria, mail day sharpened my loneliness.

"What did you get?" I sniffled. Alie had something from her partner and her sister, including a facial masque packet from the drugstore, to help cleanse her pores and have a laugh, I supposed. Alie immersed herself in reading. I was glad to be in the tent with her where it was okay to cry, especially since I felt like a spoiled drama queen. I sat up, let the tears flow, and wrote in my journal.

I started a letter to Dalton. At first, I wrote in generalities, then marked the page with an asterisk: "I don't know if I will read you this next part... I am so happy everyone has letters, and I am grateful for my package... But I was hoping for something from you." It reads like a passage from an Elizabethan novel. The page was so wet I had to scatter the words across it, wherever the ink would stick.

I had started to fill the cold afternoons and stormy mornings with fantasies of home, an explorer's crutch. I imagined the people I loved and the scenarios I missed most, like fireplace evenings or warm baths and a bowl of summer berries, but I tweaked those waking dreams beyond perfection. I added Dalton's cabin and woodstove, his steadfast, calm presence, but I took away the jokes I didn't find funny and his endless need to talk over every detail. Even as I missed him, the real him, I knew there was something beyond reality about it. It *would* measure up sweetly when I got home, but it wouldn't last. Right then I didn't care. I missed him because I missed comfort, and I didn't mind a few compromises to soothe my Arctic sores. I would sort it all out later.

Once I'd dried my tears, I read through the packet. My best friend from my middle school days reminded me not to pick my mosquito bites (a terrible habit), and her husband, a board game lover and competitive Scrabble player, included a few sketches from Pictionary cards for me to guess; one was definitely "baby teeth." A girlfriend included a list of

"Top 10 Reasons Why Getting Your Ass Frozen Off in the Arctic Is Better than Being in Victoria," and my mum wrote lots of proud mum stuff and tried to imagine my experience. The biggest surprise was from my dad, a retired news producer who wasn't much for talking about feelings. He made his letter extra tiny and sealed it with Scotch tape. He'd written it on a narrow page that read "Things To Do" across the top—the kind of pad you get at the dollar store:

"To do!…

Live for each moment and be a part of all that surrounds you.

Blend into the land and feel the heartbeat.

Feel the earth and water and let your presence blend as one with all around you.

Let it spread out until you and all around you are one.

Then pull it back into the concentrated life force which is you.

Practice this whenever you can find a quiet moment, and soon, like those 3-D images we can see by looking through the patterns, you will be able to retreat into a oneness with all around."

My dad actually wrote that.

My favorite letter was from my granny, who was ninety-two at the time. She had immigrated to Canada from England at age sixteen after finishing a middle school education and going to work for a tailor. In Canada, she worked as a cashier until she met my grandfather, whom she outlived by twenty-five years. When I was growing up, I split my time between three houses. I lived mostly with my mum but sometimes with my dad and also with my granny. In some ways Granny's was my favorite; it was always the same. Her toast was the yummiest, I got through my homework early, without a fuss, and never had the bad dreams that dogged me at the other houses. When I had a stomachache, she soothed it with a spoonful of milk of magnesia that came from a mysterious blue bottle, old enough to have come with her from England. I liked that Granny put butter in my peanut butter sandwiches and wrapped spongy homemade cookies in Saran Wrap. At night, she would come into the tiny bathroom and sit her slender frame down on the toilet seat so we could talk while I was in the bath. Her house didn't have a shower. Bath times lasted until I was almost a teenager and old enough to stay home alone. When I got my first boyfriend, Granny was the first family I told; ditto the first time I got drunk. I could trust her with any secret, and she would never complicate something that could be simple.

By 2005, dementia was encroaching on her mind but not her spirit. Her note came on a rich piece of creamy paper that she had likely saved from a special notepad. It was three inches square and read, "Jenny. I hope you are having a wonderful trip. Love Gran. June 1st, 2005." She liked to put the date on everything.

We didn't talk about the mail too much, but it changed things a little. Alie cried while she paddled the next day— from homesickness, I supposed, but I didn't want to ask. In the absence of any real privacy, sometimes you have to construct some. Her tears reminded me that she had come into our group without knowing anybody very well, so she probably missed her friends back home a bit extra. I was too nervous to ask Tim what it was like to get a letter from his dad but not his mom.

In some way, the letters buoyed me up and reminded me that I was loved. Everyone, except Granny but including my friend's husband, reiterated that sentiment, but several people also tried to imagine where I was and what I was doing or feeling—my mother more than anyone—and they all got it wrong. Of course they got it wrong; how could they know? But those letters indicated a reality of my wilderness-bound life: most of the people closest to me would never see me in the places I love most, where I am often at my best and sometimes at my worst. The separation between my outdoor life and home life had already begun by 2005, because I had started guiding professionally in remote places and taking trips far away from my wider community. The gulf would continue to grow after the trip, when I started working deep in the temperate rainforest of British Columbia, out in the bush of the Northwest Territories, and across the Arctic into Greenland. There was no overlap between home and away. I spent more time with bears than with my closest friends. Although I sometimes yearned for home, I felt restless once I got there, and I moved a lot.

When those letters arrived on the Back River, I felt both loved and forgotten. Both feelings gave me freedom. The letters snipped another thread between me and them, here and home. In a counterintuitive way, the mail increased my commitment to the river. Every day, every event demanded something new. More attention. Less resistance. This trip had a big cover charge, but I began to think we had paid it.

✳

IN THE DAYS after we released the Dead Girls' canoe, our path and the caribou's tangled together. The caribou became those people you run into in the neighborhood; you're delighted to see them, but you never know which encounter will be the last. Your overlapping patterns won't endure forever, and you know that. The day you don't see them will turn into a week and then a month, and you'll never be sure whether they moved across town or simply changed their schedule. As with the girls, we had been on a collision course with those caribou all along. Although we never knew how far the animals spread around us, we learned that an empty riverbank could fill in minutes. I wondered whether we had ever been just one hillside away from them before.

On the third caribou day, the number swelled further, and some grazed right at the river's edge, where we could take a closer look. We floated 25 meters away. Tim took a picture of me from behind against a backdrop of animals. I snapped one of Alie when she turned to face me, like a rock concert picture with the band in the back. In some places, the males with big antlers gathered, separated from the mothers and young. The sound! We hadn't been close enough to hear it before. Thousands of hooves clacked and squished as they hit the ground, and the legs them-selves, the feet, added to the din; with each step an adult caribou takes, a tendon slips back and forth over bone, and it fills the air with the sound of fingers snapping. In the foreground, little calves, far from their mothers, would chase each other—tails straight up—and pounce from

Caribou midsummer. CREDIT: TIM IRVIN

springy legs. Mothers keep track of their babies by calling out constantly, and the little ones whine back. When the calf is ready to eat, as we saw over and over, he dashes back to the udder and bashes his head against it, again and again. All of this amid coughing and snorting and the ever-present wind.

As the herd slowly moved across our field of view, the edge emerged, along with its stragglers. The ones not likely to make it to winter. The outliers who would die from exhaustion or age, though a wolf or bear was likely to pick them off before that. We had seen stragglers already. One or two would run crazed along the river's edge as they searched, against minuscule odds, to find their herd again.

A caribou in mid-migration looks more like a hungover survivor of a bar brawl than a symbol of wilderness and freedom. In summer, the herds that travel together are called a post-calving aggregation, and they move, sometimes in huge groups, back to the tree line, where they spread out again. Their thick winter coats haven't yet covered up the summer's damage from exertion, stress, and the torment inflicted by parasites. Bald spots, scratches, and holes turn their dull brown fur into a record of injury. Dark circles surround their eyes, even the calves', and their snouts are black as soot. Ribs press against the skin. Caribou are punished by so many insects that they sometimes perish from a slow drain of blood. Mosquitoes and blackflies hound them until they snap from the torture; some will run miles to get away. They also have to deal with more sinister specialists, including the warble fly, whose larvae burrow under the skin of the caribou's belly and crawls across the ribs until it gets near the spine. There, it cuts itself a breathing hole and makes a wet nest, where it feasts throughout the winter until late spring, when it pops out, pupates on the ground, and emerges as an adult fly the size of a bluebottle but without any mouth parts (it has already eaten enough for a lifetime). Populations can reach into the thousands *on a single host*, but they may be less disgusting than the nasal bot flies, who deposit live, active larvae into the caribou's nostrils. Those larvae spend the winter in their host's throat, and by spring they've made a tight mass of maggots, which the caribou try desperately to eject by coughing and sneezing. Finally, by hacking like a tuberculosis patient, the caribou hurl the larva to the ground, and the cycle starts again. Caribou are the tundra's Job. They might be a spectacle of nature's power, but they are no less a miracle of survival.

Finding those animals was a dream come true for me, and it was tempting to imagine a deeper meaning. I had prayed hard for a caribou to cross my path until I saw how that desire was holding me back from appreciating the rest of the journey. So I let it go, which I hated doing, and then they appeared. It sounds like a lesson from a book of daily meditations—*let go and your deepest desires will come true*—but it isn't. The tundra cuts a person down to size, disabusing us of new age notions that we are at the center of it all. That alone is a good reason to go there.

✳

WE STOPPED AGAIN to walk into the hills and watch. This time, to my surprise, Jen, Alie, and Drew stayed at the boats while Tim, Levi, and I walked on. They would barely see the caribou from down at the riverbank, and I couldn't understand why they didn't want to spend more time watching them. We had talked about it being a once-in-a-lifetime opportunity, a first for all of us, but perhaps it had been enough for them already.

The three of us found a huge boulder to lie on, shoulder to shoulder, and we passed the binoculars back and forth. Zoom in. Zoom out. I felt a little bit like one of those caribou, except my herd was small. I had grown strong but tired, bug-bitten, and hungry. Given the length of the caribou's journey and ours, I wanted to stay together with the herd for a while. I wanted it for myself and for Tim.

Once Tim had come to terms with leaving his dad alone for the summer and decided to continue with the trip after his mother died, what he wanted and needed from the tundra became extra important to me. I wanted to smooth the road for him somehow, though I couldn't articulate it at the time. Because of what he had been through, I thought his opinion about a group decision should carry more weight than the others'. If Tim didn't give his opinion, which he often didn't on that trip, I would guess or consult with him privately and then stick up for that point of view. I had been to the hospital and the funeral and seen his father's spirit burned up by grief. If our trip had some healing to offer, I would try to find it. If popularity was the price, so be it. I felt protective of Tim, and it could make me impossible to negotiate with on seemingly trivial points of group process. "We need a rest day." "We should stop checking the time." "We came here for the wildlife." Oh, I could be stubborn.

Tim and I talked about the trip and his grief during our time alone. He loved to watch the wolves, muskox, and bears; he hated to rush; he wanted to rest. In the city, I would have taken him a bouquet of flowers or food for the freezer. On the tundra, I tried for moments.

My approach, which I never thought rationally about, likely caused more harm than good. For one thing, we had a long way to go and couldn't afford to stop on every whim. For another, grief keeps its own counsel and won't be bullied. It's an emotion that must be accommodated—it moves in with you for a while—and all we could do was make room.

I felt peaceful tucked between my two friends, but we had the rest of our herd to think about. The others were likely trying to be patient; it was cold after all.

"Should we go back?" I ventured after a long time on the rock between my friends. I didn't want to and knew Tim wasn't ready. He would have sat there all day, joined the herd if he could. His pace was out of step with that of a group trip, in which compromise, especially about timing, is inevitable. He was already thinking of the seven-week trip he would take three years later all by himself. That way, he would never have to bend to anyone else's schedule. He could follow every fascination, and he would. "Finding those caribou was one of the most fortunate things that had ever happened to me," he told me later. "It was hard to be with people who didn't share that."

Spending time with us made him dream of spending weeks alone.

We packed up and left the caribou behind, sort of.

Later that day we pulled out to scout a big set of rapids, another pinching-in of the river. Our shoes sank into the sandy banks. Curved, parallel white lines that mirrored the lapping of the waves contoured the beach. The lines were thin and bent and beautiful, but I didn't realize what they were until I crouched down.

"Ring around the tub," said Tim in amazement.

Caribou hair, from thousands.

I swore I could still smell them.

CHAPTER 13

ARRIVAL

Those caribou days ticked by in a wash of beauty. The weather stayed clear and warm with enough breeze to discourage the bugs. We tackled the rapids and whooped and hollered as we nailed each line. We ate dahl, burnt popcorn, spaghetti, molasses cookies, bulgur hash, pizza, vegan macaroni and cheese, and walnut chocolate chip bannock. We fished, and it was hard to catch something small enough to eat. Long sunsets bathed us all in candlelight for hours each day. We were starting to look weathered; we were earning our stripes.

I had reached the part of the trip that had felt unattainable a month ago. I believed that I could hike, paddle, and lift big packs out there forever and not be tired. I became wiry and wide awake. I imagined that my eyes were clear; I could have used the compass mirror to check, but I didn't. Life was more beautiful with nothing to reflect it but the water's surface.

Although the land had doled out so much large-scale drama, the comfort of that week made it easier to appreciate the little things. We found gyrfalcons, who spend the entire winter up north; peregrines on cliffs, ready to chase down the smaller birds they hunt for food; and even two bald eagles, hundreds of kilometers from their usual range. Ptarmigan chicks scuttled through the dwarf birch. A woolly bear caterpillar rippled over dry soil. Delicate black casings of warble flies shone like onyx between the bushes. By an Arctic fox den, the adults broke stolen eggs in the midnight sun, and pups squealed while the yolks streamed gold onto the ground.

Going on personal trips, as opposed to working as a guide or naturalist, helps me reconnect with the mysteries of the land. I can forget the specifics of a ptarmigan's nearly continuous molt that helps it blend into the tundra every season. I don't need to remember that woolly bear caterpillars live seven years before turning into moths and that Arctic foxes steal goose eggs to feed litters of up to eighteen young. On my own trips, I don't have to answer why the wolves are howling, how many bears are in the area, or what someone else should wear that day. I still pick up the field guide, but I spend more time outside the boundaries of my knowledge.

WE'D BEEN ON the river a month, and because of our night paddling on the lakes, we had stayed on schedule. We were into the biggest rapids by then—Escape, Sandhill, Wolf, Whirlpool. Eddy lines boiled into dangerous traps, and whirlpools sucked at the air. My arms felt like no match for the waves that slopped against the hull and fuzzed the land with their rush and roar, but I was ready to take them on anyway. I loved the tilt of the boat as we powered into an

Scouting Wolf Rapids. CREDIT: TIM IRVIN

opposing flow and leaned all the way over in unison. I knew the weight of our boat and how it would react to each challenge from the river. I still suffered from a pounding heart and pre-rapid nausea—the stakes were as high as ever—but we were hauling ass, and it was fun.

I stretched at the river's edge while we scouted the second of the Escape Rapids. This set was straightforward, meaning not technical or windy, but the water was gigantic. The waves in midriver stood 7 or 8 feet tall, much too big for open boats in the most remote corner of the Arctic mainland. A sharp rock turned up a diagonal curler so pronounced I thought of Hawaii—except the water here was black.

After scouting, Jen and I returned to the boat, where she took the bow, and I took the stern. Time to review the plan.

"Are you good?" I said to her.

"Straight ahead, river right, avoid the curler and the rock, eddy out."

"Perfect."

We let go of shore and let the river take us, as it wanted to. We accelerated—"Power! Power!"—into the tongue, and I overrode that part of me, always a little part, that wanted to grab the shore and wait (for what?).

The diagonal push that came from left to right tried to slam us back to shore. The wind would assist, but I pried us out, mid-tongue, until we moved beyond the black-on-black shadow that waited to toss us over. It passed a hand's breadth from my hip, and we were home free, for one... two... until I angled toward the boiling eddy line. Chaos. Too much angle and we would sprawl over instantly, too little and it wouldn't let us in.

Fortunately, adrenaline gave us extra strength. Jen reached across the boiling confusion and planted her paddle like a tree in firm soil. She leaned far over, beyond logic, and our whole vessel pivoted around her until we bumped up gently to the head of the eddy. Joy surged through me.

"Nice!"

Jen had the knack: trust, lean into it.

Farther downstream, an expanse of granite, inches above river level, served as both kitchen and dining room. Our last onion, from the girls, fried on the stove. My mouth watered. Tim and Drew spent a long time casting for the perfect lake trout. Tim filleted and battered it while its flesh twitched. Jen stirred the onion and added some pine nuts.

Pink swirls embedded in the rock curved under our feet as we settled a short distance from the stove, eager for our bowls. I had been off admiring the pink river beauty flowers in low light. My plastic bowl arrived, heaping with quinoa, onions, pine nuts, and crispy trout. The batter crunched between my teeth; the tundra hadn't yet stolen its heat. The fish steamed; onions sizzled. We savored the food and licked our bowls clean.

Jen and Tim returned to the kitchen area, and I closed my eyes. Moments later, they were back.

"Oh my God," said Drew.

I opened my eyes to find a golden cake, home-dried apples and bananas, and a pan full of melted chocolate.

"Fondue!" Jen exclaimed with a grin.

The river slapped behind us as twelve hands scooped cake and fruit into hot chocolate, then scraped every morsel from the sides of the pan. My stomach stretched blissfully.

The next couple of days proved to be rare weather gems: sunny, warm, and calm. We couldn't help but feel the same way. In the city, every tangle with a friend or colleague must be overtly dealt with or silently buried. It was different on those cold, sweeping plains that made us feel both small and strong. Often, a dispute or cranky spell had more to do with when I last ate than anything more complicated or emotional. And the land governed our moods just as much. Just as crossing the ice had scrubbed away tension and the storm had forced us even closer together, so the beautiful days— with the sky wide and blue—made for peaceful travel and easy friendship.

We decided to camp early and pulled off a big ferry to river left, where we found ourselves in a jungle gym of granite. The water had dropped enough to expose shelves of layered rock that jutted out into the river and provided seats and countertops. We spread out to explore and relax, and then Alie came over holding the packet of facial masque her sister had sent.

"Do you want to join me at the spa?" she asked.

How could I refuse?

Tim and Drew didn't want to play, so Alie, Jen, Levi, and I met on the warm rocks next to a little pool of water. Jen and Alie took charge.

"What do you have in mind?" I asked.

"Foot rubs, hand massage, hair brushing, facials—you know," Alie smiled.

The awkwardness I would have felt doing these kinds of things back in the city hung on for a while, but I soon relaxed into relaxing. Jen dabbed a poultice of oatmeal and peppermint tea on my face, while someone else put my head in their lap and brushed my hair. I didn't even know we had a hairbrush. Rubbing each other's feet took some courage, but it felt great. Levi took special care to check that my toes—still swollen and purple from too much cold and wet—weren't getting worse. He massaged, salved, and bandaged a stubborn crack in my hand. A bit of extra time and effort turned a lazy afternoon into a luxury. At the end, we all lay in a row on the rocks and sighed. When I washed the cracked oatmeal off my face, my skin did feel smoother.

We pulled out all the stops that night, and Drew built a tiny campfire with his precious stash of driftwood. We ate by its glow.

As dessert was cooling, Levi walked over to the river but rushed back a few moments later. He called to us in an urgent stage whisper, "Guys! There's a caribou making a hairy ferry!"

We all stood up to see, and sure enough, an adult male with a huge rack strained against the current. Caribou like to cross at narrow points, but this animal was making the same scary ferry we had made earlier to reach our campsite. The rapid had one smooth tongue at river right and a huge ledge beside two big, nasty holes at river left. The caribou had waded in and started swimming when Levi noticed it.

We stood up in time to see the caribou cross the smooth water with his body perfectly angled for a forward ferry. His scoop-shaped hooves pedaled the water below the surface. He was a third of the way across when his eyes darted to us, and his nostrils flared with a snort.

"We should hide," said Tim, even though the animal had clearly seen us.

We crawled along the bank and ducked behind a group of boulders. As I left the kitchen, I grabbed the fresh cookies made with oatmeal and salvaged butterscotch chips and passed them out. It was time for some high adrenaline Arctic TV. We sat behind the boulders, munching our dessert and awaiting the outcome. We had clearly spooked this caribou. He needed a plan.

He didn't want to come to our side anymore, but he didn't change direction either. Perhaps he had fled a predator or was too simple or stubborn to go back on his decision. We watched as that lone animal played tug-of-war with the river at the top of the tongue, where the current was fastest. With each pedal of his legs, his head lifted higher out of the water and ruffled a wave around his neck. He kept the same angle, so the more he pedaled, the closer he inched toward us—above a bone-snapping hole that would surely tear him apart. Even the smooth line led to a wave train 6 feet tall.

The caribou sustained his position in the river for the time it took us to eat one cookie. Then the slip began. The caribou strained, and the river pulled with a smoothness that belied its power.

"How is that possible?" Jen asked aloud for all of us. A canoe wouldn't last a second trying to pull against that force. It had been minutes.

By then, each kick slipped the buck an inch or two back until the froth nipped at his backside while his nostrils widened and his eyes panicked.

"He's going into the hole," someone whispered.

"It's our fault."

We stood up together and ran toward the river, though I had no idea what we would do once we got there.

I wondered if there would be blood, but that caribou's last surge of power carried him out of the death trap and down the rapid's dark throat. He maintained his line and rode the wave train, backward, like the pro he was. After riding three massive waves, he pulled enough reserves to cross the eddy line with a good angle. He hunched in the slacker water for a brief moment with his chest heaving. Then, without a backward look at us, he scrambled up the steep slope on jelly legs. We sat speechless until he disappeared over the rise.

"WOO-HOO!" Drew yelled finally. "Way to go! Yeah!" He turned to us. "He's fine!"

✳

THE CLOSER WE got to the river mouth, the more difficult it became to find a route with white water small enough for our boats. From a distance, the waves that rose to the maximum we could handle were barely visible against the monsters that dominated river center. The trick was to keep perspective. It would have been easy to bite off more than we could chew, and sometimes we wanted to. Those smooth vees and clean waves enticed us. If we could have had warmer water and a car in the parking lot, we might have tried them. Instead, we reminded each other of a critical paddling maxim Tim and I had learned years before: *Never let desire overwhelm your better judgment.*

Those major rapids posed similar challenges for George Back. As another furious white-water hole dragged his boat into the abyss, one of the crew lost hope and began to pray. Steersman McKay, remembered for his skill and level-headedness yelled, "Is this a time for praying? Pull your starboard oar . . . Heaven helps those who help themselves,"[1] and they managed to escape disaster at Escape Rapids, as Back so aptly named them.

Nine white wolves greeted them at Wolf Rapids, and at Whirlpool Rapids they were borne along so swiftly "that it required our extremest efforts, the very tug of life, to keep the boat clear of the gigantic waves below: and we succeeded at last only to be tossed about in the Charybdis of its almost irresistible whirlpools."[2]

British naval officers were required to keep written accounts, which were often published, and the pages of their journals are riddled with niceties about sponsors and fellow officers. For example, Back named the large lake at the end of the river after Captain Sir John Franklin, a man he didn't like. He said Franklin's name would always be associated with that part of North America, and little did he know how right he was; Franklin died near the mouth of the Back thirteen years later, and the precise fate of his expedition has yet to be discovered.

If I had read Back's account before running the river, I doubt I would have put much stock in his descriptions of the white water, but I would have looked more carefully at the landmarks and tent rings, many of which were occupied by Inuit families during Back's voyage. With so much talk about exploding population levels these days, we don't spare much thought for landscapes that are emptier of people now than they were in the past.

By July 29, 1834, after one final shoot of white water, Back entered the Arctic sea. "This then may be considered as the mouth of the Thlew-ee-choh, which, after a violent and tortuous course of five hundred and thirty geographical miles, running through an iron-ribbed country without a single tree on the whole line of its banks, expanding into fine large lakes with clear horizons, most embarrassing to the navigator, and broken into falls, cascades, and rapids, to the number of no less than eighty-three in the whole, pours its waters into the Polar Sea."[3]

Their adventure wasn't over yet. They still had the coastline to map, and even when they reached their farthest point, they were only halfway home.

With his 30-foot boat and ten men, Back traveled from the Baillie River to the river's last rapid in fourteen days. It took us twenty-nine. If we had been on the river the same year—rather than 171 years apart—we would have met up close to the coast around the end of July.

✳

ON DAY 37, Franklin Lake met us with broadside waves that made paddling tedious and Jen seasick. Luckily, the weather held, though the barometer was beginning to drop. We went to bed in a state of suspense, but the next morning was still beautiful. As usual, we asked Levi to account for the conditions; he shrugged and said, "The weather is a many-variabled variable."

In the morning, we stopped after a portage, only our seventh of the entire trip. Tim headed off to try to catch some char—his final challenge as an Arctic angler. By that point, he was throwing most of the lake trout back. "Too easy," he said. The rest of us stripped down for a swim. We took advantage of the heat and indulged in some naked time on the rocks. We took silly photographs in which we showed off our muscles. When we took to the water again, Jen decided she would be warm enough with just a PFD and a pair of pants.

The map showed one more set of rapids before the beginning of the delta.

As we approached it, several things vied for our attention. First, the river narrowed dramatically from over 2 kilometers wide to only 400 meters. Second, a group of gigantic inukshuks stood out against the sky. Third, the entire bay before the rapids was thick with a herd of caribou geometrically larger than any we had previously seen.

We headed for the bay.

The grunting reached our ears first, followed by the clacking of hooves on stone. What we had seen earlier in the trip was repeated and magnified. I estimated that there were ten thousand caribou. They shook the land with their soundtrack and pulverized it beneath their feet.

The scene around us that afternoon summarized the expedition. In a landscape that swallowed giant herds and then revealed them like rabbits out of a hat, we also found monuments, mysterious to our untrained eyes, from the people who had come before us. The river cut between all of it and gave us a path to follow; others had followed it, and still more had attempted it, but water makes no trails and so lets you feel like the first visitor. The rapids ahead represented the physical challenge we had faced throughout our journey, and the unknown crouched around each corner. Through all of it, we had been six dots of color in three little boats—red, green, and blue—who had promised to go all the way together.

Our campsite would be fairly close to where the caribou were roaming, so Alie suggested we go make camp, and those who wanted to come back to the caribou could. I couldn't imagine preferring to leave. And there are never guarantees with wildlife, no matter how settled in they appear. Tim and I exchanged a look, but we carried on to scout the first rapid.

We could see two sets, and we could tell from far away that the second was much too big to run. So the first set in this final rapid would be our last of the summer. We put all of our training to the test: scout, review, position, run, recover. The current carried us as if we were cycling on an open road and moving fast enough to risk a painful fall. We ran it like pros and then bounced out of the boats for big hugs and congratulations.

We lugged the gear up to the campsite, and Tim and I headed back toward the caribou. Their hoofprints had turned the shoreline into braille, and they were gone. I was sorry to miss them but glad they had left us as mysteriously as they had come. In the half hour it had taken us to run the set and come back, they had funneled to who knows where.

We climbed up to the inukshuks and tried to figure out how old they were. Huge blocks, bigger than a person could lift alone, balanced on each other to make figures taller than any of us. Large circles of lichen, which grows only a fraction of a centimeter each year, sealed the rocks together. George Back would have stood near these very inukshuks in 1834. When he arrived at the final rapids on the river, he met a group of Inuit who gathered in a semicircle around his boat after his men brought it ashore. What began as a fearful encounter soon became friendly after Back, by his account, used his limited Inuktitut to declare peace. The rendezvous shifted to hand shaking and gift giving—Back distributed fish hooks, buttons, and beads, and the Inuit gave the men tools and small objects they had made.

The very last rapid was enormous, a perfect curler set between two gates of rock, 400 meters apart. A black trough of water flashed steeply into a series of standing waves nearly twice my height. We took portraits of each other there and ate supper on the spine of one gate, so close to the water we shouted to be heard. I had the strange impulse I've sometimes felt at the edge of a cliff; I had to concentrate to keep myself from leaping off.

Our campsite perched above that rapid, another threshold we were about to cross. Things would be different on the other side. For one thing, salt would soon tinge the water. And although most of the journey was behind us, the most uncertain part still lay ahead. None of us had tackled the Arctic Ocean before, and thinking about it shifted the baseline. The river that had been so unknown now felt like familiar territory. We had risen to its expectations, but soon we would have a new master.

We spent the evening playing rodeo with the waves. We started by throwing rocks; then someone fetched the Pelican case from the Dead Girls' camera, tied a rope to it, and threw it into the maw. As the light faded—it faded toward midnight by then—we took turns holding each other by the belt and heaving our little surrogate into the water.

"Ride the hole, baby! Ride the hole!" Tim yelled as the case took violent drownings, one after another.

CHAPTER 14

CONTACT

The next morning, as we headed for the Arctic Ocean, we spotted four yellow tents, one beige tent, and three canoes off to our left. I heard the woman before I saw her.

"Hi there!" she shouted across the river.

We grew nervous. We had almost forgotten how to greet a stranger and weren't sure that we wanted to; the solitude had become familiar. We contemplated not stopping at all, but the woman was insistent. *Why is she being so loud?*

We changed course and headed in.

"Where are you from?" she called.

As we got closer to her waving arms, I could see they were both wrapped in gauze. One hand was enveloped in a bright white mitten.

She chatted but did not refer to her condition. A second woman clambered down from the tents to reach us. This was George Drought's party, the second woman said. Drought was a well-traveled Arctic paddler who had met Levi in Toronto and given him a series of annotated maps of the river. We had been following his arrows and triangles for weeks. That day, he lay in his tent with facial burns and possible lung damage. The woman who greeted us was his wife, Barbara. Her chattiness was a product of painkillers.

George and some of his clients—he and Barbara guided trips in the summers—had been cooking oatmeal inside their massive beige "tundra tunnel" that morning. When Barbara came in she noticed right away that the stove didn't sound right. It hissed below a large pot, the one they always used, but the windscreen wasn't in the correct position and the fuel bottle sat too close to the flame. She walked over to the stove, and as she reached for the pot to remove it, a loud boom erupted as the bottle burst into flames. Fire engulfed the tent. It vaporized the roof and blasted George's face with a fierce heat. The flames melted most of Barbara's pants and shirt from her body—she immediately started picking the melted plastic from her skin. Her chest, legs, and arms, now exposed to the air, began to blister, but her left arm was much worse than the rest of her body. She headed to the water to cool her burns, while one of the clients, an emergency physician from British Columbia, treated George for shock and tended the wounds on his face. She worried that he had inhaled the heat into his lungs. One other man had minor burns on his hand, but everyone else in the group of eight was okay. The physician then bandaged Barbara's arms—the left one was already swelling like a football—and gave her morphine tablets for the pain.

We arrived an hour later.

While we sat dazed and drifting, listening to the physician's story and wondering what to make of the bandaged woman in front of us, the rest of the group waited for a Medevac. The helicopter would arrive shortly to take Barbara and George to the closest medical station, in the town of Baker Lake. The remaining members of the group were comfortable enough to complete the last three days of the trip on their own.

After thirty-nine days on the tundra, these were the first people we had seen. If we had arrived two hours later, they would have been gone. We asked how we could help: Did they need food? Help carrying something out? Someone to stay for a while? A phone? But the only help they needed was hundreds of kilometers away and approaching fast. Another point for satellite technology. As I later read on the Widjiwagan website, "Camp is literally just a phone call away." Technology makes us feel as if we aren't so far away after all. It tethers us to the perceived safety of home, which alters the psychology of a trip, but it's more than psychology; George and Barbara were about to be saved.

There was nothing to do but keep going.

We stopped for lunch an hour later. We yanked crackers and oily cheese from our lunch barrel as the helicopter flew over our heads.

THE OCEAN REACHED our noses by midafternoon. The ripples on the water had subsided and created glass conditions, but the sea hung in the air all day. We camped 20 kilometers from the delta that would officially empty us into the ocean, but we had already started dipping our fingers over the side to taste for salt.

We had been running tough rapids and traveling every day for almost two weeks. We were slightly ahead of schedule, which I wasn't thrilled about. I would have preferred time to hike and explore than go full steam ahead for so long; however, I couldn't deny that the ocean was a big unknown, and we were better to err on the side of caution with our schedule.

The string of good paddling days had tired us out, and the next morning we slept an hour later than usual. I woke up feeling sluggish and impatient. We needed a break. I waited for breakfast and checked the map. The farther we got into the sandy delta, the less accurate the maps would be. We needed to stay in a main channel, but the ribbons of the river curved in all directions.

After breakfast, Drew gathered us together. He was Leader of the Day that day, but we didn't usually need to meet.

"I'd like everyone with their paddling partners today," he said. He explained that we were heading into bigger water with a bigger margin of uncertainty and that it would be best if we stuck to our most reliable teams. This was not an unreasonable idea, but something in the way Drew delivered the instructions set me off. He was Leader of the Day—a role designed to ease the group process—not Dictator of the Day. It was not his place to give us instructions.

"Are you *telling* us who to paddle with?" I asked.

"I guess I am. I think it's best."

Drew's plan was motivated by emotion rather than logic, or so I thought, and I didn't want to obey him. Just like the day Tim and I crossed the river to find the girls' camp and he tried to stop us.

Anger constricted my chest, and although I tried to stay calm, I wasn't very successful. I said that it was not his role to give orders and that his orders didn't make sense. It was these small things that ignited maximum frustration in me when fatigue set in. "Fine," I finished petulantly, and Jen and I loaded our boat.

We had an upwind battle that day, and rain soaked our collars. We stopped twice, once to fill a barrel with water before the river got salty and once to visit a hunting cabin surrounded by wolf skeletons—which hardly cheered the mood. By completing the final rapid on the river, we had entered a zone that could be accessed by oceangoing motorboats. People from the small community of Gjoa Haven—our final destination, still over 200 kilometers away—could visit by boat as well as snowmobile. The cabin contained fresh plywood and notes from winter travelers.

By 4:00 p.m., we had called it quits. Drew made the final call on a campsite, which was a dismal choice among bad options. Flat, boggy, barely above water level, and covered in goose shit.

"Goose Shit Island," Jen called from the bank.

We wandered around in the muck. No one felt committed to it, but paddling was not much better than sleeping in the silt and poo.

Levi spoke up first.

"It seems a shame to choose this site. It won't be good for a day off or a weather day if we stay."

I could see Drew was thinking carefully about this. He tended to give Levi's opinions extra weight.

"We could pack up and paddle on," Levi continued.

Oh boy, I thought, *here we go.*

Levi kick-started a discussion: why to stay, why to go. Drew was inclined to agree with Levi, even though he had made the call to stop—and for the second time that day, I was annoyed. Levi's word had come to mean more than anyone else's, and that upset me. Tim had asked Drew to stop calling our rotating leadership position the Levi of the Day, saying "we all have expertise to contribute." Tim and Levi were equally strong paddlers, four of us had northern experience, and we all had good problem-solving skills. Levi didn't need the extra authority, and he didn't want it. Yet one sentence from him could change everything. That night, because of Levi's hesitation, Drew might have asked us to pack all our soggy bags again and head off in search of a less terrible site. In a delta.

After needless discussion, in which Tim said nothing and I took deep breaths, we stayed. The calm, sunny days felt like years ago.

Alie and I cooked that evening, and my irritation simmered. I wondered what the highlights of this trip were for Alie, but I didn't ask. Lately she seemed keen on as much sleep as possible, and I could think of better places to go on a relaxing holiday. Our cooking styles didn't match either. We were like dance partners out of step, always treading on each other's toes.

At least Jen and I were getting on okay, or so I thought.

I decided it was just one of those days—which I have more often in the city—when it's best to go to bed and try again tomorrow.

✳

THE OCEAN GAVE itself away by turning our surroundings from silt back into rock. We burst from the river on Day 41, and the landscape snapped from shallow soil to scoured stone. Salt clung to the air and to the shafts of our paddles. The water took on a new blue, despite the overcast sky. A north wind blew, but not too strongly, so we tucked behind an island and headed out into the thick of it. The rock around us, while flat and scrubbed, appeared as if through a prism: white, pink, gray, green. We reached the little island by lunchtime, and got out to take a look and have some food.

The eastern side, where we landed, formed a low peninsula that we could easily crest to look north toward our goal. The island sloped up on the west side to form a smooth dome, striated by glaciers and too inhospitable to let much plant growth develop. By the time we finished our bannock, the wind had strengthened. Time to camp.

Drew, Tim, and I started with a wrestling match. We tackled each other to the ground and laughed amidst a flurry of fake side slams and piledrivers. It lasted until Drew's wicked elbow drop accidentally connected with my face and sent a gush of blood from my nose. I sat down in a patch of lichen and staunched the flow with a handful of wet moss. Tim took a photo for posterity and to show everyone back home how tough the trip really was. Then we set up the tents and climbed into them. We slept for three hours, until it was time for supper.

"It will be hard to make the distance out here," Levi observed over dinner.

"A small wind for this place is too much for us," Tim said.

We sat around the stove and contemplated our new position. Jen picked at a seam of micalike rock. The polished stone all around us was shot through with lines of different color and consistency. Too bad none of us knew anything about geology.

"Good thing it's a nice island," I said.

Drew headed down to the water to do the dishes. He had used pure water from the barrel for tea but brackish water from the ocean to boil the pasta. We sat in the mixing zone where fresh water from the river floated on the surface, but it wasn't pure enough to drink anymore.

I woke the next morning to Drew's voice outside the tent I shared with Levi. He called out in a high, whiny falsetto, "Housekeeping!" Levi and I burst out laughing. "You want fresh water?" he continued. Amazing that I could be so irritated by someone and then like him so much in the same twenty-four hours.

The wind hadn't died at all overnight. We weren't going anywhere.

After a pancake breakfast, I took off on my own to explore the island. It was shaped like a turtle. Its rocky head jutted east into the waves and took ten minutes to walk across. The sandy neck housed our kitchen and food cache, and we traversed it hourly to gauge the wind. Our tents were tucked into the turtle's right shoulder, from which its shell rose smoothly. I climbed to the top of the island and looked east, where the massive sandy plain of the Back River delta looked two-dimensional, like an aerial photograph. Some of that sand, molded by a labyrinth of waterways, had traveled as far as we had. Silt from the banks of the Baillie mixed with soil knocked loose by

Back's boat in 1834. By the time the Inuit moved into the watershed, that delta had already been building for centuries. Below me, lumps of granite rose from the ocean like the backs of whales in white, pink, and black. The weather and glaciers had beaten the surrounding cliffs and peninsulas into animal skins; they looked like zebra stripes and shadows on a cheetah's flank.

I took a few hours to explore all the way around the island. I hadn't seen anyone but my companions in more than a month—except for our odd encounter with the Burned People—but I still needed my alone time. You can spend weeks in the solitude of the tundra without ever being alone, or you can arrive home to realize that you didn't spend *enough* time with someone from your tiny group. For example, even in our society of six, I rarely kicked around camp with Jen; we paddled together, but usually only on days with wind or white water that required focus. We spent a lot of camp time in a group, so closer bonding with one person didn't come easily.

The island was perfect for a solo adventure because of its relative safety. I didn't think about bears or getting lost. I picked a few samples of plants to look up in our field guide and found a small pond out of sight and out of the wind. I watched the cotton grass bob and wrote in my journal until I got sleepy. I would return to that pond many times over the coming days.

Nothing had changed with the weather by the next day. Drew's group journal entry joked about our predicament:

Future note for ocean paddlers: if you don't want to drink from puddles then don't camp on an island. There are no lakes on small islands. Just lots of big rocks and small rocks and flat rocks and pink rocks. We even had to move some rocks in order to tie down the canoes! It's windy out here folks!

We had committed the ultimate rookie move by stranding ourselves mid-ocean with no source of fresh water. Tim and I hauled a barrel up to some of the rainwater ponds and filled it using a bailer. With a huge stretch of water between us and our final destination, the wind had us well and truly stuck. We made the most of our time as the hours became days. We slept a lot, played Boggle, looked for mountain sorrel to nibble on, and stood on the windward side of the island watching the impressive whitecaps. I read three books. Progress was out of the question. Jen and Tim reached new heights in camp cooking with the invention of bannogies (bannock pouches filled with instant potatoes and cheese) and a date-apple-chocolate-banana-walnut pie of sorts. One morning, we sat around long after breakfast discussing the true meaning of forgiveness. Then we got out the kite.

A kite is the perfect toy for an Arctic trip. It is small and light and needs the very thing you don't: wind. We flew our zippy two-handled kite high over the island and crashed it into the granite over and over again until it was too crippled to fly.

Those days on the island gave us time to rest and maybe too much time to think. Tim's grief caught up with him there. We hadn't had supper yet; it might have been seven o'clock. The sun slanted toward the horizon, a destination it would reach in three or four hours, but the days were getting shorter by then. I approached Tim's tent and met the sun's glare at eye level. The bugs weren't bad, but I still paused by the tent door to take off my jacket and untie my boots. I yanked the zipper, dropped to my knees inside, and stuffed my jacket in the corner while kicking off my boots and rolling all the way in—my hand already closing the mesh behind me. The sun pressed the yellow walls, thickening the air and releasing the damp from Tim's sleeping bag.

Tim lay on his right side with his chest to the wall; he was sobbing again. *I don't want to be near this anymore*, I thought. The clarity of my inner voice surprised me. Tim gulped the heavy air. I almost walked out on him, hating him for the heaviness that had followed us all that way. I lay down beside him while he cried into his sleeping bag. The light in the tent was hazy, and I imagined the Dark Cloud of Tim, pushing down on us, reaching for me. I didn't blink. I would wait the requisite few minutes to show that I cared and then get the hell out of there. The comforting made no difference anyway. When I sat up, I looked over at Tim's face and saw that he looked very thin. His flesh had been sucked away by forty-four days of labor and hard grief. I squirmed out into the vestibule and pulled my boots back on. Sun glared at me from the rocks. Dry stems clung to my clothes—Tundra Velcro, we called it. I set off to rejoin the others.

EVENTUALLY, THE SUBJECT of getting home crept into our discussions. We'd been on the island for four days. We couldn't help but think about our departure, but had no idea how or when we would get home. Levi had started checking the wind at all hours of the night and puzzling over his barometer. Our original plan was to get picked up at Montreal Island (two-thirds of the way up the huge inlet we had just entered) by a boat from the community of Gjoa Haven—we had commercial airline flights back to Yellowknife later in the month—but perhaps there was a better pickup spot that we could reach back at the river mouth. The phone gave us so many tantalizing options for creating a new plan, getting information, controlling the situation. But the land cannot be controlled.

We decided to wait. And cut down on our food consumption.

CHAPTER 15

HUNGER

D uring the days on the island, I often thought about food. The longer the expedition and the hungrier you get, the more engrossing a topic it becomes. After a month and a half, I had pages of notes for a book on the subject. The slim volume would be about food preparation for wilderness expeditions. I brainstormed the chapters and listed diagrams I could draw of different stove setups and cooking fire techniques. I would compare modern and historical meal plans and relate the backstory of expedition food, including pemmican and limes to prevent scurvy and the trade routes that supplied early trips with cocoa. Recipes would share pages with photographs and personal stories. Titles would be pithy and ironic: Principles of Baking and the Poofiness Factor, 101 Things to Do with Bannock, Food Disasters: Cream of Wheat.

Food provides a thin cushion against forbidding uncertainty. There is comfort in homemade granola and fresh-baked bread, and confidence in the kitchen breeds confidence on the river. I learned that the hard way on my first long trip with Tim, in 1999. When we packed for the trip, we measured out healthy portions of everything, but we didn't use any guidelines. We eyeballed it. We made a rotating menu and simply added everything up. I remember counting out the salt: 1 tsp + ½ tsp + ½ tsp + 1½ tsp ... Unnecessary hair-splitting arithmetic, but we didn't know how else to do it. We found some recipes in old camping books and invented others. I came up with a particularly vile formula for curried rice and raisins. Out on the river, hunger settled in after the first week. Our snacks did not match our appetites, and they tested my honesty. From the bow, when it was my turn to split up the trail mix, I resisted scooping most of the M&Ms into my share: *If I take more than half, he will never know.*

On the sixth day of our trip, while paddling across blustery Lake St. Joseph, a motorboat pulled up beside us. A gorgeous blond fishing guide with a ponytail and mirrored sunglasses shot us a smile. He had his dog in the boat with him. I suddenly felt shy about my bed head and dirty T-shirt. "You want a tow?" he said. The wind was almost too much for us. I threw him the bowline but forgot that three pairs of my underwear were tied to it so they could dry on the bow deck. The flimsy cotton panties flopped into the water, and I fumbled desperately to untie them while my face turned bright red.

That night, the guide, Bruce, fed us moose steaks and leftover coleslaw from the fly-in fishing lodge where he worked. I thought he was only slightly less cool when he put on a cassette tape called *Jazz Loon.* The next day, he showed us around the place, took us fishing, and sent us away with some leftovers and an extra can of naphtha gas for our cook stove. Despite my vegetarian tendencies, memories of the moose meat only piqued my hunger over the next few days as we kept to our menu of Alfredo sauce from the Bulk Barn and couscous so dry we had to focus not to aspirate it.

By Day 12, it was time for a treat. We deserved it, and I wanted to surprise Tim with something special. I pulled out our only stash of chocolate, a package we kept in the wannigan along with our cooking gear. A few chocolate turtles, some peppermint patties, yogurt-covered raisins, and one extra-large bar of Lindt milk chocolate with hazelnuts hid between pots and cutlery. I spread a sampling on our Frisbee along with a sprig of fresh wintergreen and brought it to the campfire.

The chocolate tasted like pure energy, and it promised to return flesh to our bones. Flavor saturated my tongue. At least two minutes passed before I started burping. My gut began to lurch and vapors dried the back of my mouth, but I refused to look up. We each took another piece and ate in silence. Finally, with mounting digestive upset and corrosive breath, we met each other's eyes and faced the truth. The chocolate had been contaminated by naphtha from a leaky fuel canister. Bruce's gift was, in fact, a curse.

"Could we eat it anyway?" But we knew the answer. We'd have to burn it all, the only free, extra calories for many miles.

We dumped every morsel into the fire. Flames wrapped the glistening chocolate. Sugar and gas accelerated the blaze. I actually shed a few tears over the funeral pyre.

We burped naphtha for two days after that.

We were so far behind schedule that we skipped our re-supply and survived on half of our already inadequate rations. I remember pausing in the middle of a windy lake to choke back powdery soy nuts and chickpeas. Sometimes we stopped for guilty spoonfuls of peanut butter, hoping we would have enough to finish the trip. And that was before I got Giardia, aka "beaver fever." That tenacious intestinal parasite got to my food before my body could absorb it and kept me running over the banks and into the bushes up to ten times a day.

Tim eased his hunger by imagining, out loud, the most extravagant ice cream sundaes. "Three scoops, no, four scoops. Chocolate, chocolate chip, Rocky Road, caramel."

"Stop it. Seriously," I grumbled. My hunger was best contained by silence or distractions. His word paintings of hamburgers, pastas, milkshakes, and sandwiches made everything worse.

We survived that trip by catching walleye and buying a few groceries from the limited and expensive selection when we traveled through the Ojibway community of Eabametoong, also called Fort Hope. Outside the store, we ate a container of strawberry cream cheese in one sitting. When we ran into fishermen further along our route, we would hang around and casually mention our food issues until they tossed us a bag of dried fruit or some biscuits. At one fishing lodge, a couple of women who ran the kitchen invited us in for tea. They put out a plate of fresh-baked cookies, and we ate them all before the ladies even sat down. Later on, when we got really desperate, I orchestrated a stakeout. We had met some anglers who were flying out the next day, so we took a detour to casually camp across from their cabin.

"This will never work," Tim said, but I felt confident they would have castoffs. I piled our campfire high that night, to make sure they saw us, and waited into the dusk for them to come and drop off their leftover groceries. Tim finally went to bed, hungry but smug. "I told you," he said. I had to admit defeat until I heard the drone of a motorboat early the next morning. I grabbed my clothes and darted out of the tent, trying to look casual.

"Good morning!" I called to the man in the boat.

"Our plane is on its way. Thought you could use some of this." He unloaded a full box of food. Bingo!

We lounged for the rest of the morning over Nutri-Grain bars, scrambled Egg Beaters, corn muffins with fresh butter, and instant vanilla coffee.

By the time my dad picked us up on the Ogoki River in August, I was down to 122 pounds from my usual 140. We were skeletons with big grins.

※

ON OUR NEXT long trip, in 2002, Levi was particularly worried about our food rations. He had found a book about a trip on the Dubawnt River, *Death on the Barrens* by George Grinnell, and he read it as a cautionary tale. It had frightened him.

"We've got to bring enough," he would say every time we met to discuss the trip. "We're going to burn a lot of calories, more than you'd think. We need to plan for that."

He asked everyone in the group that summer to read it, and the book became part of our tripping lore, one more stream in the watershed of our experience. Grinnell's story is a memoir from his troubled youth, and it reads like a psychological thriller. It is hard to say how accurate his version is, but as young paddlers, we were affected by his words.

It was the summer of 1955, and three canoes sat by the shore of Black Lake, Saskatchewan. Arthur Moffatt's group of six men, including him, aged thirty-six, and five others, aged eighteen to twenty-two, had been trying to leave for a week. The food shipment hadn't arrived, so they replaced three months' worth of provisions with whatever they could find in the village of Stony Rapids. Then they forgot three paddles and had to go back to town for them. The weather kicked up, and the overloaded canoes took on water every time the group tried to embark.

"There's no hurry," Moffatt said, "we've got all summer."[1] But they had no idea what they were in for. They would need every possible day if they were going to make it down the Dubawnt River to Baker Lake, 1,400 kilometers distant, before cold and hunger overtook them. The only other non-native explorers who had traveled in that area, to their knowledge, had been Samuel Hearne in 1772 and the Tyrrell brothers in 1893.

Arthur Moffatt had experience on northern rivers like Ontario's Albany, which he'd paddled alone at age seventeen and subsequently guided several trips on, but this Dubawnt odyssey was more ambitious. Privately, he wondered if his group was up to the challenge. His second-in-command, Frederick Pessl, called Skip, had traveled with him before. So had James Franck, the youngest paddler and the most practical (he was the only one who carried matches in a waterproof container, according to Grinnell). Bruce LeFavour, the second youngest at nineteen, had brought along his reluctant college roommate, Joe Lanouette. These two would be the bowmen, along with George Grinnell, whose book would later etch the journey into the minds of paddlers everywhere, for better or for worse.

Moffatt's crew of young men came from different walks of life, but they had one thing in common: when they went North, they followed their leader. But as the pre-departure days dragged on and the delays continued, the men grew restless. "If I were superstitious," said Skip, "I would almost believe we were not meant to go down the Dubawnt."[2]

Moffatt often thought of his family back home. Before he had kissed his wife and two daughters goodbye for the summer, he had doubled his life insurance policy.

It was 7:00 p.m. on July 2 when they finally pulled away from shore.

The first portage took a week. Caribou trails led off in all directions, and the Canadian Shield created rocky barricades as Moffatt's men stumbled through a maze of small lakes and tangles of scrubby spruce. They struggled with heavy loads and battled an onslaught of blackflies and mosquitoes. Progress was painfully slow, and Moffatt, who had been feeling "sad, apprehensive and gloomy about the summer,"[3] continued to worry. He recorded this in his journal, parts of which were later published in *Sports Illustrated* magazine. The physical work punished him. His neck strained from carrying his 39 kilograms (86 pounds) of movie-camera equipment on a tumpline around his forehead, and he pulled so hard on the strap that even when he lay down at the end of the day, his elbows wouldn't straighten.

They weren't far from Black Lake, just shy of the Northwest Territories border, when the hunger began. Pickings were slim and monotonous. They had a hundred bags of oatmeal for breakfasts, dry pilot biscuits with peanut butter, jam, and cheese for lunch, and, every day, a dinner called "glop": two boxes of Catelli macaroni, two tins of tomato paste, two packages of dehydrated soup, two cans of Spork or Spam, and one gallon of water. Other simple stores like mashed potatoes, onions, and prunes provided the only variety.

Moffatt cooked most of the meals and distributed all of the rations, but after the first two weeks, the men grew hungry before, during, and after every meal. They circled the supper pot each night and tried to snag the largest pieces of meat with the ladle. Only tea and sugar were not controlled, so they'd drink cup after cup until Moffatt made new rules. After that, they wet their spoons to snag more sugar crystals. They stopped sharing their extra snacks and tobacco. Peter Franck began saving pieces of his biscuits in old jam containers. The oatmeal sat in canvas packs and grew moldy.

As July gave way to August, food supplies dwindled and tension grew. At the same time, a strange peace settled over the group. Grinnell was perhaps the most affected. He came from a wealthy but troubled family and had served in the military before joining the expedition. Possibly because of this, he considered himself physically superior to the other men and didn't bring gloves or a warm sleeping bag. He followed Moffatt into the wilderness, he wrote, because he wanted to change himself, to "be born again, strong, courageous, heroic, self-sacrificing, obliging, witty, in general, the most loveable person in the world."[4] By August, Grinnell and most of the others had succumbed to a sort of delusion. They felt they were in paradise. As the food in their packs diminished, some became convinced they could sustain themselves with wild foods. Two of them had brought guns and started hunting caribou, while others fished or gathered berries. The wild feasts were like a holy communion for Grinnell, but the season of plenty in the North is painfully brief. Winter was already galloping toward them.

The days grew shorter, but instead of pressing his team onward, Moffatt took long walks in the morning, filmed, and stayed up late at night. It seems nothing—not hunger, lack of provisions, increasingly cold nights, or the caribou's southward migration—could rouse him. According to Grinnell, only Peter Franck kept a grip on reality and urged the group to keep moving. Nobody would listen. For half of August, they voted to take "holidays" and went nowhere.

By August 29, three days before they'd planned to complete the trip, they had traveled barely half the distance. The caribou were long gone, the weather changed overnight, and the men were trapped on the land. Dreams of plenty were a thing of the past. The remaining caribou steaks were "full of grubs and cysts of one kind or another," wrote Moffatt. He dreamed more often about home, but refused to take the blame for their food situation. Skip and the others had taken back some control over rations by then. Moffatt insisted that "if I had been able to cook all meals, there would be no problem."[5]

By early September, Grinnell was entertaining thoughts of deserting the expedition and dying on the tundra in the arms of the "wonderful mother earth who gives birth to us all." He wrote that "death in paradise seemed preferable to life in civilization."[6] But his wilderness ecstasy alternated with panic attacks. He feared for his life.

The men were still over 300 kilometers from Baker Lake when it started to snow. Moffatt began filling his diary with lists of supplies and meditations about his family. He'd passed through paradise and found something darker on the other side. On September 10 he wrote, "We're all running scared."[7]

Four days later, all three boats plunged over a waterfall the paddlers hadn't bothered to scout. Two of the boats capsized. Only Franck and Grinnell stayed upright. Moffatt and his bowman had been in the water the longest, but the other two swimmers, Skip Pessl and Bruce LeFavour, were being swept downstream, so Grinnell and Franck rushed to them first. By the time the rescue was over, Grinnel had also fallen in the water, and Moffatt was severely hypothermic.

On shore, Grinnell unpacked a sleeping bag, removed his own sopping clothes, and climbed inside. Before falling unconscious, he remembers calling to Moffatt, "Get undressed and get in this sleeping bag with me."[8] But Moffatt was too cold to move and Grinnell too weak to help him. By the time Grinnell awoke, Franck had started a fire using his waterproof matches, put Moffatt in another sleeping bag, and attempted to resuscitate him. It was too late.

The survivors spent the night in each other's sleeping bags, nearly frozen to death. The next morning, they laid Moffatt's body under an overturned canoe and sprinted, half-starved, toward Baker Lake. They paddled big lakes and shot dangerous rapids, covering 300 kilometers in eight days. The day before they reached town, they ate their last meal—the remainder of a jar of curry powder, split five ways.

When the five young men stumbled into Baker Lake, an RCMP officer made a quick assessment: "So," he said, "you lost your sense of reality."[9]

✳

LIKE ANY MEMOIR, Grinnell's story has been criticized. Everyone has a different reason for committing a journey to paper, and no one has the same memory. Whatever the truth, Grinnell's account helped solidify Moffatt's posthumous reputation for incompetence, perhaps unfairly. Like most disasters, the outcome was the cumulative result of mistakes that can only be tallied in hindsight. But the story, aside from encouraging us to bring lots of nutritious food, made me think about the expectations we bring to the wilderness. Perhaps these men's first mistake wasn't a lack of material supplies. Maybe they fell victim to the trapline of stories and stereotypes we have created about the northern landscape: wilderness as healer, transformer, provider, paradise.

CHAPTER 16

STANDBY

he temperature hovered between 8 and 11 degrees
Celsius during our days on the island, and the
wind blew steadily. There was no question of
going anywhere, so there was no point in getting impatient.
We stayed huddled in our extra layers and amused ourselves in our little granite universe. Levi began checking the
wind more and more often. He finally had to admit that he
couldn't control the weather with his barometer.

Early on the fifth day, the wind had died enough to
quell the whitecaps early in the morning. We made a break
for it: packed the tents, downed some gorp, loaded the
boats—but the wind came up again. We reversed the process and set up camp once more.

We were tired from too much rest, so we played Sardines
(like hide and seek) and Land (which involves throwing
sticks). By lunchtime, Drew, Levi, and Tim were sitting
next to each other and lobbing rocks at the lunch bucket.
First one to get a stone to stay on the lid wins. We were
running out of things to do.

Drew suggested we use the Dead Girls' phone to call our contact in Gjoa Haven, Charlie Cahill, and we agreed. It was Charlie's job to organize a boat charter to pick us up from Montreal Island the following week. The agreed-upon date was fast approaching, and we were over 100 kilometers from the pickup point. The least we could do was give him a heads-up. Drew retreated to the tent to get away from the wind and start a conversation with the outside world.

Through the tent wall I heard the hellos and then Drew's surprised question: "Ice?" he said. "Do you think it will blow out anytime soon?"

My breath caught in my throat.

Drew emerged moments later. "Gjoa Haven is completely iced-in," he told us. "There aren't any boats on the water."

At first, I thought the ice was already forming in Gjoa Haven, that winter had begun. But during the first week in August, the villagers were still waiting for spring breakup. Too late for snowmobiles, too early for boats.

"So nobody can come and get us until the ice blows out?" Jen asked.

"He said that the ice is really late this year," Drew replied. "It normally breaks up by August 4." I laughed. It was August 8.

Drew explained that Gjoa Haven needed a strong north wind to clear its harbor, but it was the north wind that kept us stuck on the island. The village needed something stronger, but we couldn't move until the wind dropped.

Charlie suggested we continue north when we could. As an afterthought, he mentioned that we should keep our eyes open for a family near Montreal Island. They were running out of food, and he was trying to get a helicopter out to them. Another group whose trip wasn't going as planned—this time, because of ice and weather.

After that call, we had more information, and although nothing had really changed, it made us feel like we needed to *do* something. We would spend a long time yet discussing what could be *done*. It didn't seem possible that the answer was nothing.

We skipped dessert that night. No more extras.

Levi awoke at four o'clock the next morning, and conditions looked promising, but within an hour, whitecaps crowned each wave. Alie and I did an inventory and discovered we had twelve days of food left. We decided to call Drew's dad and start researching options for flying out. Given our ignorance about the behavior of sea ice, seeking outside advice seemed like a good plan.

We pulled out the girls' phone. Its one battery still worked, but the battery symbol showed only one bar out of three. There was no spare, and the battery couldn't be swapped for the fully charged one in our phone. I agreed that we should make the call and then regretted it. In case of an emergency, we would need every drop of power. Drew promised to keep the call short.

＊

WE HAD APPOINTED Greg our safety coordinator back in the spring. At the time he was the vice president of IBM's Global Services, a job with huge responsibility that called for a tech-savvy leader who could be reached at any hour. Greg is logical, reliable, and organized. He also loves canoeing and had done some short trips closer to home. We had promised not to call unless there was an emergency, so two weeks before, when he and his wife had received Drew's first phone call late at night, he'd imagined the worst. Our second call, on August 9, wasn't as shocking. Rather than feeling scared, he felt activated. We were iced-in and needed ground support. Greg was on the job.

He established a command room in the den of his house and dispatched Drew's wife, Hilary, to buy several huge maps that covered Gjoa Haven, Montreal Island, and Chantrey Inlet. She laid them all out on the floor while Greg fired up two computers and got on the phone. *I need to understand the situation,* he thought. He started with the temperature, wind, and barometric pressure in Gjoa Haven. Then he contacted Charlie Cahill and anyone else in the village who might be able to help, including local RCMP and the wildlife officer. He also reached the air charter company in Yellowknife, ice analysts at Environment Canada, and, eventually, all of our parents.

※

MEANWHILE, OBLIVIOUS TO the flurry of activity we'd triggered back home, we headed to bed. The next morning at 2:30, the beginning of our seventh day on the island, Tim, Alie, and Drew stood on the shore looking north and assessing the conditions. The wind was still blowing—but less so. Perhaps it was dying, though it was hard to tell in the dark. They decided to wake us up.

"We're going for it," Tim said from outside our vestibule. He ruffled the nylon. "Let's go, you've been sleeping for a week."

After a quick handful of trail mix, we were off.

Orange began to fringe the horizon as we bobbed up and over each wave. The sea had subsided somewhat but not entirely. The sun rose from the water, above where I imagined the delta; it touched our cheeks, promising warmth. I fixed my eyes on the water horizon and set my arms in motion. We had spent six days on that island, and we needed to move. I hoped the wind wouldn't force us back to camp again.

We hit a rhythm and didn't falter. Every minute took us north, and with each passing stroke, the water flattened until we floated through a calm so complete it was hard to believe the transformation. From a relentless storm, stillness emerged.

We stopped for more food and the coffee ritual that Jen and Alie couldn't do without. We ate lunch on the water and had a quick conference about shortcutting across a large unnamed bay. The weather seemed stable—though we'd been wrong before—but we needed to make progress. We decided to go for it. During the afternoon, the separation between sea and sky vanished; water appeared above us, air below. Silver and blue. Our rhythm dropped only once, when a ringed seal broke the surface. We swiveled around to each other, mouthing, "Wow!"

A week off had weakened us. My arms burned by midday, but we had to keep going. We paddled well into the evening, until we'd made half the distance to our endpoint, about 50 kilometers. We'd barely spoken since morning. A shallow pan of sedimentary rock settled for home that night, inches above high tide. Tim took his boots off and waded, heronlike, into a shallow pond in search of drinking water. Silt billowed at the slightest disturbance, and little water critters darted every which way. Tim walked forward at a smooth pace and dipped the bailer into every clear spot he could reach, but zooplankton still flicked around in the barrel when he brought it back to camp.

We slept for four hours with a mixture of peace and anxiety that the wind would return. I awoke with sore arms and a crinkly, sunburned nose. A slight headwind rippled across the water, and I prayed it wouldn't build. We had at least another 50 kilometers to go, so we packed up and pulled away from shore at 4:00 a.m.

The headwind gave us pause before a second huge crossing, this time of Elliot Bay. As with the day before, we had planned to trace the shoreline for safety's sake, since the wind could pick up anytime and leave us unprotected out there. But the crossing would save us at least 20 kilometers of zigzagging and island hopping, and we couldn't resist. Levi checked the barometer one more time— "Steady"—and we agreed not to stop at all on the transect, not for seals or photos or because of fatigue.

Jen and I chatted to pass the time and somehow came around to communication styles and team dynamics. I think Jen surprised both of us when the conversation hit a nerve. Sometimes a person simply needs an opening, at the right time, to get something off her chest. It turned out that this woman—who had emerged as a cheerful force of optimism, who had become an incredible camp cook and solid bow paddler and had brought so many smiles to Tim's face—well, she had some feedback for me, and she couldn't contain it anymore. I wondered if the vast ocean and the canoe, where we didn't have to look at each other, made it easier for her to open up, the way a long drive on an open road can.

"You take up all this space in the group," she said. "You talk over people; you don't give us room."

I stayed quiet.

"You don't listen. And I don't feel like we make decisions together about how to paddle the rapids. I want to learn, but I'm not included." She paused.

"And you always get what you want but in a roundabout way. You're subversive about it; you manipulate people."

That last point hurt the most.

When she was finished, we let the rhythm of our paddles carry the conversation for a while. No way to take a break from each other and no way to stop traveling. The saddest part for me was the timing: Day 48. *We could have done something about this.* It had all built up for too long by then.

I resisted the urge to defend myself. She was right—a little angry just then, but not wrong. I had been impossibly stubborn at times. I had been pushy, though I hated that it had seemed manipulative to her. As for the white water, I hadn't wanted Jen to see how it pushed the limits of my ability. If I was scared shitless, I didn't want to pass that on to my partner. Sometimes, getting through safely took all of my focus.

The rest of my sadness was more private. It had been a challenging trip for all of us, and I had paid an extra price by feeling caught between Tim and everyone else. It was a lonely place to be, which Jen probably didn't know. I watched Tim joke and play, and I was thankful to see his good mood increase bit by bit over the summer, but I also saw his ragged edges more than the others did. It confused me to be one step removed from someone else's grief. I had loved Tim's mum too, and I had been on the sidelines through the aftermath. In our eighth week of collective solitude, the six of us had been through so much, but that afternoon I realized what the costs might be. I had bulldozed Jen and the others sometimes. I had sacrificed some friendships. That is how I dealt with being a neighbor to grief.

The conversation ended well. Jen said her piece, and I absorbed some of it, shed a few tears, and let the rest sink into the water. One of the tundra's lessons came in handy that afternoon: carry on, carry on.

A growing shadow of silver helped steer our attention to other matters. The sea ice Charlie had warned us about was on the horizon. Two hours later, our boats crept between the ice floes.

Jen turned to face me. "Our first sea ice! It looks different than on the lakes."

It wasn't like the freshwater ice we had seen earlier. Each floe stood a foot out of the water and sank about three feet below. Many chunks had snow layers on top. Each section of ice defined itself clearly, without any of the mush we saw on the lakes, and when the pieces hit each other, they thudded. None of the tinkling we had heard upstream.

We stopped on the Adelaide Peninsula, which Levi immediately termed a "bulbous isthmus." The wind had dropped again, and we were further shielded by the ice, so the protected water north of the peninsula formed a heavenly stone-skipping pond. And the beach was covered with perfect stones.

I would have loved to lie in the sunny curve of the protected bay, but time was no longer on our side. We pushed

Final days. From left to right: Jen, Drew, Levi, Tim, Alie.
CREDIT: JENNIFER KINGSLEY

through the ice for the rest of the afternoon, the day's odometer clicked past 50 kilometers, and our final destination, just north of a small stream and across from Montreal Island, came into view. There was no sign of the family Charlie had mentioned.

"Land ho!" Drew called. "We are almost there; we can do this!"

As if conjured up by Drew's optimism, the wind awoke. Within ten minutes, we could hardly make headway. It took all of our strength to gain the small beach of our final destination. By the time we secured the boats, the conditions had grown too dangerous to paddle. Wind chopped the waves and pinned us in place.

We had done it.

Jenny on Day 52. CREDIT: DREW GULYAS

"We're here!"

"We made it!"

We jumped and hugged each other. Jen and I held each other's arms and smiled. "Thank you," I said. We shared a tent that night. Perhaps it wasn't too late to make amends.

We had traded the ice-choked headwaters of the Baillie River for this icy bay. When I went through the motions of setting up camp, nothing felt more natural. I knew how many tugs it would take to free the nylon from my pack, and I flicked the tent poles out in a perfect arc to snap all the pieces together. I had achieved a sense of home; yet as soon as we landed at our final campsite (or so we thought), our objective changed again. It happened in an instant. For almost two months we had put our all into getting to that patch of ground. Now it was time to think about leaving altogether. Part of me was ready—past ready—but the rest of me felt rooted and unwilling to go.

✳

GREG HAD BEEN busy in Toronto. By the time we settled in near Montreal Island, he had two ice forecasters assigned to his case and was getting updates twice per day. He had begun reading digital ice maps and interpreting satellite images. He had chosen an aircraft to charter and was on a first-name basis with the owner of the air charter company. His inbox and phone hummed with messages from our families. Their responses ran the gamut. Tim's dad sent an email far and wide to friends and family about our exciting situation: "Ah, the balance between adventure and danger!!" he said, and recommended that everyone buy a copy of Alie's upcoming book. On the other end, at least one parent called Greg, nearly demanding that he send the plane and offering a blank check to cover the costs. That person's opinion was clear: "Let's get this done."

Fortunately, Greg was not easily swayed from his mission, which he and Levi had thoroughly discussed before our departure. Greg had clear instructions from us about locations, dates, and contingencies. Any changes to our final exit plan would be ours to make, not his, unless circumstances dictated otherwise.

✳

SOMETIME DURING OUR forty-eight-hour marathon, Levi had discovered how to send and receive text messages, which used less battery, and communication with Greg became part of our routine. Drew let slip that his dad had stopped going to his job at IBM so that he could work out the logistics of our exit. We started to get daily updates like "Gjoa Harbour 90% coverage, ice 4 ft. thick."

In contrast to Greg's hectic life in the command room, we had nothing to do but wait. I started yet another book— we had all read most of each other's by then—and explored the stream by our camp. Drew and I headed up the stream together to find some good drinking water. We chatted a bit about the trip, and I was amazed to realize that in fifty days, Drew and I hadn't talked one-on-one or paddled together very many times. I admired Drew for his courage and spirit, and I wanted to know him better. The river had changed all of us; we'd grown stronger and somehow shinier, but it showed more on him. I watched him stride over the slippery rocks with a barrel on his back and realized he had found his footing.

Near a riffle upstream, we discovered a fox den. Hard-packed earth, full of holes, mounded up above the permafrost. There wasn't any activity, so I walked a few steps to the top of it and found a goose foot lying in the dirt. I picked it up and worked its rubbery joints with my fingers until Drew joined me. If we stood very, very still, we could hear the pups' tiny yips and moans underground.

The next morning, as I leaned against the wannigan with a cup of tea in my hand, wolves slipped between the tents where everyone else was sleeping. They seemed to take everything in: me and the boats, the ice and the shadows, but if they made a sound as they blew through camp, I couldn't hear it.

I wandered over the rocks and stopped to stretch my arms above my head. The air on my belly felt good. I climbed a small rise and looked north to check the progress of the ice. It had moved in overnight. When everyone else got up, I shared the news: "If that ice gets much closer, we could get too boxed in here, even for a plane." It made sense to move to the island itself; we hoped one of its many bays would stay open.

Greg was poised to fly us out, which would cost more than $8,000. If he didn't hear from us again, he would default to sending the plane a few days later, but we still had to make a decision for ourselves about how and when we wanted to end it. We could hold him off, wait it out, stick to the plan. Or we could get out while the clear weather lasted.

We packed our gear and crossed a kilometer or so of open water to set up camp behind two small islands. Upon our arrival, we received another message from Greg: "Move 1.5 km south into shelter of two small islands." Exactly where we were already.

Later that day, another directive from the phone: "Do not attempt to swim to the mainland."

"Do not attempt to *swim* to the *mainland*?" Tim repeated when he read the message. "Does he really think we would do something so ridiculous? We just paddled the most badass river in Nunavut. We're not idiots."

"That's my dad for ya," said Drew with a smile. "Captain Obvious."

I could see the disconnect between Greg's information and ours. He had satellite images and weather reports, and we had our senses and our wits. He wanted to send us helpful information, but his information was our environment. Our brief and broken conversations were attempts to bridge the gaps between his imagination and our experience, but the gulf was too wide. Yes, we were pinned in by sea ice and unsure how to get home, but we were warm, dry, fed, and not about to make a break for it by swimming. I cringed to think what some of the other parents and partners might be thinking. A text message on dying batteries, no matter how well crafted, wasn't going to calm anybody. Without the phone, we wouldn't have had to make a choice about how to leave. Our phone and PLB were supposed to be safety measures. They provided security, both practically and psychologically, but I had never contemplated their true power. They could threaten the very experience we were looking for.

Once a desire to get home took hold of some of us, it became increasingly difficult to wait. Drew wanted to be home with his wife, and Alie was also ready to head south. Even Tim was tired—not so much of the place, but of the trip and the group. Jen and I were supposed to be bridesmaids at a mutual friend's wedding in Toronto a few days later, but I still had mixed feelings about the decision to leave. My commitment to the original plan stayed strong. I felt like I was cheating on the river to think about leaving it. Levi was the only person who wanted, 100 percent, to wait out the ice and leave by boat. While some held a clear position on what to do, most of us, at least some of the time, felt unclear. It wasn't so much that the group was divided, but that each of us was divided by our conflicting desires. It was a test of stamina to let the land decide our fate when we could take a semblance of control with one phone call. With that final decision, to fly or not to fly, we tested the bounds of consensus-based decision making. We considered every angle. The expense of the plane and the worries about food and ice were just the beginning. What about the poetry of our voyage, the commitment to see Gjoa Haven, and the execution of the boat exit? What about the fossil fuel emissions, the environmental ethics?

When we ended yet another discussion in stalemate, on Day 51, I grabbed the soap and headed to the beach. I stripped my clothes off into a stinky heap and marched into ice water that stabbed my ankles and thighs. Waves splashed the thin skin of my belly and squeezed my lungs and xylophone ribs. I would not let the ocean force me out. I would wash my hair, even as the water cinched a band of steel across my forehead. I tried to relax my neck and stop thinking about home.

CHAPTER 17

OVERTIME

On Jen's birthday—August 15, Day 52—we all took a walk together. With the end in sight, we clung to each other, despite our indecision. Every meal, hike, or sleep could be the last, depending on the ice. We passed a small group of caribou—there were at least twenty-five on the island with us—and I wondered what would happen to them over the coming winter. It was too late to be that far north. We climbed over granite boulders and across dry moss to the ridge looking north. The tundra's spice rose briefly to our noses before the wind snatched it away. A shiny mat on the water extended north to the horizon and, to our dismay, curled around the south of the island as well.

George Back had also been stuck in the ice upon reaching Chantrey Inlet and Montreal Island. He stood at the same vantage points we did and marveled at the shards of ice that piled up on the beach below. Back monitored the ice constantly, hoping for openings that would allow him to follow his intended course, but the risk of a gale forcing ice against his boat and crushing it was too great. "We had therefore nothing for it," he wrote, "but to yield to necessity, and wait submissively until nature should remove the barrier which she had placed."[1] When conditions allowed, he crawled north toward the Arctic coast despite constant fog and shifting ice; he badly wanted to fulfill his mission of mapping what was then a blank on the British map. He held out as long as possible, but finally the late date and poor conditions forced him to turn around on August 15. "I shall not attempt to describe what were my feelings at finding my endeavours baffled in every quarter," he wrote. "Every resource was exhausted, and it was vain to expect that any efforts, however strenuous, could avail against the close-wedged ice, and the constant fogs which enveloped every thing in impenetrable obscurity . . . even in the ordinary pursuits of men, with all the appliances of civilized life to boot, the execution is rarely equal to the conception."[2] Back assembled his men, planted the British flag, gave three cheers, and headed home.

We continued down to the shoreline, where the ice pounded the beach. Overhead, a hawk circled and screeched. The bird came low and called repeatedly into the fierce wind. About 100 meters farther on, we found her nest, where two big fledglings perched on the edge with their faces to the wind. They were rough-legged hawks, who spend the breeding season in the Arctic, and their speckled plumage blended into the rocks and sand. If they didn't fly yet, they would have to learn soon.

While we wandered the island, Greg was trying to put the final details in place for our exit plan, but he couldn't reach us. A day had passed, and his requests for a reply went unanswered. He was flying blind and didn't know if our battery had died or if something else had gone wrong. "That's when things felt like they were unraveling," he later told me. He sent messages about the ice, the boat, and the plane, but we never received them. The messages got jammed up somehow and Greg had to work with the company's IT support to clear the system and start again. By that point, he had sent six updates to our families showcasing the maps from his new friends at Environment Canada. He was amazed at what a man could get for his tax dollars.

On the island, we tried to stay in the moment, not knowing when the end would come or how. We still had a chance to call off the plane, but we'd have to do it soon. In celebration of Jen's birthday, Alie and I made a double-decker marble cake with strawberry filling and lemon icing, complete with birthday candles. We filled her tent with balloons and then piled inside to play games and drink rum. We presented her with a cardboard Bingo game we had brought for the occasion, in case we were still out on the trip for the big day. It only had a four-by-four grid, so we called it Ingo.

The next morning was our last chance to call Greg and stick to the original plan of waiting a few more days for a boat. We had been discussing the decision for three days, and by then I hated the sound of my own voice, the hollowness of my logic, the repetition of my ideas. Tim hung back a little, and I envied him his disconnect. We volleyed statements back and forth:

"If we don't get out now, we might not get out at all."

"I'm not ready to call it."

During those talks, we were no longer on the tundra. We imagined ourselves home. What if we couldn't be bridesmaids at our friend's wedding in Toronto? I had a custom-made pale green dress waiting for me at home. While I sat on a rock in the long underwear I had been wearing for fifty days straight, I could hardly imagine getting into it, but I didn't want it to go to waste.

What we had gained that summer, a feeling of being fully present—at least in moments—was evaporating. After almost two months of simplifying our thoughts and learning from the land, the "real world" began pounding at the tent flap, demanding to be let inside. The weather had turned bitterly cold, but even the wind's tug on my hands and legs couldn't keep me in the moment.

Three hours into another examination of our goals and feelings and the pros and cons of our exit options, Levi put his foot down.

"I want to stay," he said. "We have enough food, especially if I am by myself, and I don't want to go home by plane. You guys can go, but I'm staying."

I looked over at our gentle friend, appalled by this new attitude. Surely it was too dangerous. He could starve or freeze. But my arguments rang hollow. I knew he would be perfectly safe and happy, but I couldn't let him go. I wanted us to finish together; I had never imagined it any other way.

The others seemed more ready to accept Levi's plan, despite my amazement. Perhaps we could avoid a group decision after all. The idea of splitting up, of splintering, became possible for the first time, and it tantalized us.

"Is that what you really want?" Drew asked.

During all of this, Tim sat in the circle, just close enough that we couldn't say he wasn't there. He would sit in, then lean back on his elbows, listless. He hated these talks and didn't want to share his feelings. Silence would be the fastest way out of there. I loved and hated him for it.

"Do it," said Tim, finally. "Why not?"

"Wait," I said. "If Levi really wants to stay, we shouldn't just leave him here." I looked over at my friend. "I don't want you to be here by yourself. Maybe we should all stay."

Alie, Drew, and Jen sat next to each other in the circle. Their dark faces, skinny and smudged, remained mysterious to me. After fifty days, they sometimes felt like strangers.

We broke apart soon after that, knowing that if we didn't phone Greg he would likely send a plane for us in a couple of days. It remained to be seen if Levi would get on it. The bow paddlers—Alie, Jen, and Drew—left camp for a hike along the shore. Tim hung back. Levi walked back to our tent, grabbed his book, and took off across the island, away from camp. I followed him, stopping to get my own book on the way. I caught up with him as he jumped across some lichen-covered rocks, and I fell in step beside him.

"I want us all to end this trip the way we want to end it," I said, "but I don't want to leave you here." The notion of leaving him at all was unthinkable. Levi had become as much a part of my landscape as the river.

Levi put his arm around my shoulders and we continued to a sheltered spot behind some high rocks and lay down. We'd found a perfect cocoon; the sun ricocheted between the rocks, which nulled the wind, and it was too cold for mosquitoes. We lay side by side on the stones and opened our books. Come what may.

After an hour or so, a figure bolted across the muskeg, headed away from us at a full run. It was Tim.

"What is he doing?" I said.

He had his hat off, jacket open.

"Tim!" Levi yelled after him. "What are you doing?" Levi and I both laughed, and Levi said, "Does he have to go to the bathroom?"

Tim heard the calls, turned around, and ran straight toward us.

He kept repeating something, but it took a while to make it out.

"A boat. A boat. The boat," he said.

He arrived at our rock panting like a dog. Levi and I stood up to meet him. Tim threw his arms around us both, then leaned back and said, "The boat is here. It's time to go."

"No way," I said.

The three of us ran, arm in arm, to the top of the hill, where we looked down to our campsite and saw an aluminum boat pulled up on shore. Two strangers stood beside it—one big, one small.

Tim started ahead, but I tugged him back. "Wait a sec."

All of my longing to get home had disappeared.

I pulled out my camera and took a self-portrait of the three of us with our heads close together and the tundra rolling away behind us. Our last moment of the trip, in some ways. Our new leader was waiting on the beach.

It would never be the six of us again.

Levi, Tim, and Jenny on Day 53. CREDIT: JENNIFER KINGSLEY

GREG HAD KNOWN about the boat before we did. The ice shifted just in time for him to call off the plane from Yellowknife. Within twenty-four hours on August 15 and 16, he talked to the air charter, his contacts in Gjoa Haven, and the "nice ice people" from Environment Canada, and he emailed our families three times with updates. The messages read as though he were out on the land with us, and in spirit I think he was. It was hard for him to trust the final leg of the journey to a stranger, but in the end he felt that "this crossing should be as our adventurers planned it originally."

✳

JERRY ARQVIQ WAS a big man. I stood about a foot taller than him, but he still seemed big to me. He and his twelve-year-old nephew, Kenny, stood on the beach in their rubber boots. Each wore a baseball cap with the hood of a hoodie pulled over it—Jerry's red, Kenny's black. Over the hoodies they wore winter jackets; Jerry's was a parka style with a rip in the back of the right arm that went from the shoulder to the wrist. Jerry had sunglasses and a handlebar moustache; Kenny, a big smile and chubby cheeks.

Levi strode over to them and extended a hand. "Boy," he said, "are we ever glad to see you."

"Do you want some chili?" Drew asked. "It will take us a while to get ready."

In the first hour, we tripped over each other to chat with the new members of our group. How is the ice? Do you want some tea? How should we load the boats? On and on. Jerry said almost nothing, and Kenny settled in to play with our cameras and eat some supper. Our social skills felt stiff; we were out of practice. We gleaned that the last three days of wind had been enough to free the harbor in Gjoa Haven. Many people had left the village in their boats to hunt and fish, and Jerry and Kenny had come for us. There was still plenty of ice, and they had to cross a particularly wicked piece of water to reach Montreal Island.

"But you made it," I said to Jerry, "so that means the water is calm enough to cross?"

"Calm enough for us," he said, looking at Kenny, "not for you."

"Oh."

"We'll see."

"Okay. I'll go take my tent down."

Levi and I left to pack our stuff while Drew took Kenny over to start a bonfire. It had been too windy to burn what remained of Drew's woodpile, and Drew would be damned if he was going to leave before torching it. We needed time to pack anyway, and rushing wasn't really Jerry's thing.

Over at the tent site Levi said to me, "We seem pretty high-strung compared to them."

We packed our bags but kept out every layer of clothing we had in anticipation of a freezing cold nighttime boat ride. Back at the beach, we pulled the thwarts off our longest boat so that we could nest a 16-footer inside it, and Levi rigged a bridle to help tow the boats smoothly inside the wake. We stacked our bags at the water's edge for loading, and I tried to memorize the way the beach felt beneath my feet.

JERRY'S BOAT WAS an open 22-foot aluminum speedboat—the workhorse of the North—with a 75-horsepower Honda four-stroke engine. A custom-built plywood shelter took up the front third of the boat, and that is where Jerry and his family could sleep. It doubled as a hold during seal-hunting expeditions. The dashboard had a small plexiglass windscreen and a plastic ghetto blaster with a tape deck. Some fishing lures dug into the plywood next to the engine controls. All of our gear fit into the hold, and all of us fit into the cockpit. We towed the boats on different length lines behind us. Even with all of my clothes, including my down coat, I still felt the biting cold, so I hid behind

Captain Kenny (as Jerry called him), who seemed comfortable in his hoodie and ski jacket.

Jerry stood motionless at the wheel as we revved up far
faster than the six of us had gone in weeks. The evening
light was enough for him to navigate by. Kenny alternated
between filming us with our own cameras, pulling his
wooden toy boat alongside the big boat, and pointing out
birds that we could barely see. Shorebirds, seagulls, little
birds—he searched them out in the gloaming and told us
their names in Inuktitut.

As we passed Ogle Point, the water came up shallow
and the sea ice closed in. I stood up to get a closer look as
Jerry trimmed the motor and jogged between the floes. He
clearly needed to concentrate, but I couldn't stop my flow
of questions, and he answered patiently.

"I love to drive in the ice," he said. He explained that
cracks tend to open on full or new moons and that ice-filled
areas are usually navigable in the middle—you have to push
through the edges to get to the clear spots. "When the ice is
open, there is always a way through," he said, "but if it is
starting to pile up on itself, stay out." We had learned a lot
during our summer alone, but Jerry raised the bar. Our piles
of gear looked excessive. Our chatter, including my own,
grated on my ears.

"I want to teach Kenny about the ice," Jerry continued.

Darkness and ice closed in on us around midnight, and
we saw the lights of Gjoa Haven, a few miles away, around
the same time. Hot showers. Mattresses. Jerry slowly picked
his way between the floes. Kenny pushed some pieces away
with a paddle, and Jerry nudged others with the hull. The
bright ice stood out against the black water.

"Wasn't like this on the way over," Kenny said.

"I think we should go to that island," said Jerry. He gestured behind us.

But we were so close to the village.

"Or else we'll run out of gas," Jerry added.

Another chance to give up our expectations.

We found a beach on the island nearby and got out the tents. Jerry and Kenny didn't have one, and they only had one blanket, so we slept three to a tent and Levi opened up his sleeping bag to share with Kenny, who slept fine (Levi didn't).

"Wake me up when it clears in the morning," Jerry said. He stretched out on his back and fell asleep right away.

We got up early, eager to get going, and set about making breakfast. Everyone was up but Jerry. I went to his tent and said good morning.

"Is it clear?" he asked, though I suspect he knew the answer.

"Uh...no," I said. "Sorry."

Tim and I headed up onto the island's gravelly slopes in search of water. We promptly got turned around in the fog and spent an hour trying to find camp again, never mind the water.

"Couldn't find any," we explained on our return. We didn't mention getting lost.

"You don't get water from *up there*," said Kenny. He rolled his eyes a little and pointed out to the ice. "You get it from *over there*."

We strapped him into one of our life jackets and Tim took him out in a canoe to get fresh water from the snow that lingered on the sea ice. Obvious, once Kenny pointed it out.

Kenny looked nervous as he stepped into our tippy canoe. When he sat on the bottom of the boat, his life jacket pushed up around his ears. He gripped the gunwales. Tim pushed the boat into an ice floe, and Kenny set a pot and paddle down on top of it. He stood shakily and tested one foot on the ice. Solid. He eased up onto the floe—back in familiar territory—and relaxed immediately. Tim followed, and they used their paddles to shovel snow into the big pot, which Tim took back into the canoe. "Thanks!" Kenny said as he shucked the life jacket and took off across the floe in his hoodie and baseball cap.

Tim sat in the canoe and watched Kenny pull from his jacket a piece of caribou antler with a line and hook tied to the end of it. He started jigging.

"There's fish under here," he said with a grin.

The morning passed. Kenny looked around in our stuff and took selfies with our cameras, Jerry slept in, and the six of us watched the weather for any sign of change, just as we had been doing all summer.

Jerry emerged as the fog thinned enough to see Gjoa Haven again.

"I think it's time to go," he said. We loaded up.

Jerry swung his boat around the ice with ease now that we could see the path, and before we reached the harbor the ice had disappeared again. A cluster of low buildings clad in gray, blue, and beige siding made up most of the town. Gravel covered the roads and yards, and people zipped around on ATVs. The village could have been next to any number of our campsites from the summer; tundra stretched undisturbed right next door. Jerry slowed down outside the harbor and pulled out a tiny cell phone. *What now?* He grabbed the top corner and pulled out a silver antenna the length of his arm. He punched in a number and started up in rapid Inuktitut. We looked at Kenny.

"He's calling my uncle. We're pretty much out of gas."

When we finally bumped against the dock at Gjoa Haven, we were running on fumes.

I hesitated on the threshold of the boat; we would fly out that afternoon. It was time to return to showers, beds, clean clothes, family, news, cars, wallets, and fresh fruit. But we would leave much more than that behind.

EPILOGUE

I felt larger than life in my bridesmaid's dress a week later in Toronto, as if everything in the world had shrunk except for me. I had agreed to have my hair cut and to shave my legs—though that only exposed more scabs and bruises—but I refused a manicure and pedicure. I was proud of my leathery hands and cracked feet. My face was deep brown and creased, while the rest of my body looked wiry and pale. The tiny shoulder straps that crisscrossed my back felt impossibly delicate.

In the days after our return south, we sent packages to Camp Widjiwagan for the girls whose things we had collected, but we didn't hear back from them.

George Drought and his wife, Barbara Burton, received medical attention in Baker Lake—but Barbara's left arm, which she had used to lift the pot off the stove, had to be cared for at a burn center in Ontario. She wore a compression stocking for a year to minimize scarring. George did not have any lung damage, and the blisters on his face soon healed. They received a settlement from the stove company. The couple continued to paddle together until George's health prevented it. He developed Lou Gehrig's disease and, positive until the end, died in 2012.

As for the other explorers, it has been almost sixty years since the Moffatt expedition, but it still makes the pages of paddling magazines. In a recent interview, Skip Pessl, the trip's second-in-command, summed up his group experience: "People revealed themselves as imperfect. We all did."[1] For George Grinnell, revealing himself came slowly; it took him forty-nine years to complete his memoir of that summer.

In 1961, the northeastern part of Lower Garry Lake was renamed Buliard Lake so that we might remember the priest's story, but his legacy is best felt on the land and in the empty tent rings that line the banks of the rivers and lakes.

George Back was knighted at age forty-two, the same year he retired. He had been on expeditions, almost continuously, for twenty-four years. He didn't marry until he was fifty years old, after courting his fiancée, Theodesia Elizabeth Hammond, for three years. They took a ten-month trip to Europe, in which Theo described herself as a "sad coward."[2] I imagine Back journeying from one European attraction to another with his terrified wife in tow. After all that he'd experienced—from the Napoleonic wars to months of deprivation to commanding his own expeditions—how did he feel about domestic retirement with a woman like that? He outlived her by seventeen years and died at the age of eighty-two.

I knew soon after our trip that I would grow distant from three of my paddling companions, despite how much I cared for them. That true encounter with wildness, and a brush with grief, was a strain on our young friendships.

Still, every time I see a picture of Jen, she has the same beautiful smile on her face. Drew and his wife run a camp now. Last I heard from him he said, "I had no idea how that trip would change my whole life." Alie has made a wonderful success of her writing career, and Levi has migrated to the city; he's now an Assistant Professor of Biostatistics at the City University of New York and lives in Manhattan. Tim still heads to the wild every chance he gets, and so do I. We've both spent years exploring grizzly and salmon habitat on the west coast as guides and naturalists. Tim has gone back to the Arctic for two trips, including a seven-week solo, and I have returned to the North to guide.

I have only one item in my house that I brought home from the Back River. It's an antler from a young caribou, which I found on the riverbank. I brought it home as a gift for Dalton, who has remained a close friend, and he gave it back to me a short time ago. At the bottom end, where the antler would join the head, the bone in cross-section is porous and rough. The shaft of the antler feels smooth and curves gently; it is ridged by shallow canals through which blood vessels would have run when the antler was growing and covered in velvet. At its end are two prongs that head in opposite directions, and both have been chewed by rodents. If you grasp the antler in the middle and let it balance in your hand, it has a solid feeling. I have said that it's hard to keep a grip on life down here when you are up there, and the opposite is also true, so it's good to have something to hold on to.

ACKNOWLEDGMENTS

S ince our journey in 2005, this project has developed a community of supporters and committed listeners. I acknowledge everyone who has breathed life into this story.

From the beginning, thank you to:

Lynne Van Luven for inspiring me to get with the program in the first place, and David Leach for supporting me until I found the story I was looking for.

Lorna Crozier, Tim Lilburn, Karsten Heuer, Ryan Hilperts, Eric Higgs, and my classmates Scott Amos, Sally Stubbs, Garth Martens, and Aaron Shepard.

Although I needed commitment and language to write this story, one of the hardest things to find early on was a space to write in. Thanks to those who gave me a quiet place: Sherwin Arnott, Becky Cory, Ruth Nelson, Mark van Bakel, Todd Carnahan, David Leach, Bo, Jenny Manzer, and Meg and Adam Iredale-Gray.

I have half a lifetime of thanks for Tim Irvin, who never stops believing in me, even when I do, and people can do great things with friends like that. Thank you to my other

Back River tripmates for the incredible contribution they have been to this journey: Levi Waldron, Drew Gulyas, Alison Pick, and Jen McKay.

Thank you to the Banff Centre and its Literary Journalism program, including all of the 2010 participants and my admirable editors, Don Gillmor and Ian Brown.

Also:

The Canada Council for the Arts.

Martha Magor Webb (Anne McDermid & Associates), for saying yes and being a talented voice of reason and encouragement.

Nancy Flight for her clarity, care, and skill.

Jennifer Croll for her good-natured corrections and clarifications.

Rob Sanders and the team at Greystone Books for their enthusiasm and commitment.

Aaron Spitzer and *Up Here* magazine, which published portions of this manuscript.

Lake journal, which also published an earlier version of this story.

Tassy Kingsley and Bruce Kingsley, without whom I never would have stepped into a canoe.

Many people showed up at the right time and made a special contribution to this story, including Jenny S., Madeline Sonik, Heidi Braun, Jason Guille, Dalton Wilcox, Nicola Temple, Andrew Westoll, Christopher Hink, Charlotte Gill, Greg Gulyas, Barbara Burton, Ingrid Paulson, and Lesley Cameron.

The final thank-you is for Toby Meis, who has been down this river with me more times than I can count.

The mind has its own Mercator projection. The here and now retains, more or less, its true dimensions, while events from our past get pushed to the margins—stretched and distorted like the North and South Poles. For this story, I have explored the poles of my memory, and I take full responsibility for the projection that I have smoothed and pieced together in order to share it.

ENDNOTES

CHAPTER 5

1   Back, *A Long Yarn*. Unpublished memoir (up to 1819), quoted in Steele, *The Man Who Mapped the Arctic*, 26.
2   Back, *Narrative of the Arctic Land Expedition*, 99.
3   Back, *Narrative of the Arctic Land Expedition*, 61.
4   Back, *Narrative of the Arctic Land Expedition*, 105.
5   Back, *Narrative of the Arctic Land Expedition*, 109.
6   Back, *Narrative of the Arctic Land Expedition*, 114.

CHAPTER 6

1   Tranströmer, "Guard Duty," *Selected Poems*, 111.

CHAPTER 7

1   Choque, *Joseph Buliard: Fisher of Men*, 63.
2   Choque, *Joseph Buliard: Fisher of Men*, 109.
3   Groups of nomadic Inuit had names specific to the regions they traveled. Thus, it is difficult to tease out which name belonged to whom and at what time.
4   Names of groups, families, and individuals differ between historical accounts.
5   Choque, *Joseph Buliard: Fisher of Men*, 173.
6   Pelly, "The Mysterious Disappearance of Father Buliard, o.m.i.," 34.
7   Tester and Kulchyski, *Tammarniit (Mistakes)*, 250.
8   Tester and Kulchyski, *Tammarniit (Mistakes)*, 253.
9   Tester and Kulchyski, *Tammarniit (Mistakes)*, 256.

10 Tester and Kulchyski, *Tammarniit (Mistakes)*, 260–261.

11 Tester and Kulchyski, *Tammarniit (Mistakes)*, 283.

12 Tester and Kulchyski, *Tammarniit (Mistakes)*, 294.

13 Tester and Kulchyski, *Tammarniit (Mistakes)*, 282.

CHAPTER 10

1 Not her real name.

2 Not her real name.

3 Layman, "The $100,000 Rescue," 19.

4 Irvin, "Stick with the Facts," 7.

5 All quotes in this paragraph from Pick, "Paddling Back in Time," online comments.

CHAPTER 11

1 Back, *Narrative of the Arctic Land Expedition*, 127.

2 Back, *Narrative of the Arctic Land Expedition*, 133.

3 Back, *Narrative of the Arctic Land Expedition*, 137.

4 Back, *Narrative of the Arctic Land Expedition*, 192.

5 Back, *Narrative of the Arctic Land Expedition*, 143.

6 Back, *Narrative of the Arctic Land Expedition*, 140.

7 Back, *Narrative of the Arctic Land Expedition*, 185.

8 Back, *Narrative of the Arctic Land Expedition*, 186.

CHAPTER 13

1 Back, *Narrative of the Arctic Land Expedition*, 190.

2 Back, *Narrative of the Arctic Land Expedition*, 194.

3 Back, *Narrative of the Arctic Land Expedition*, 202.

CHAPTER 15

1 Grinnell, *A Death on the Barrens*, 11.

2 Grinnell, *A Death on the Barrens*, 11. Also mentioned in Moffatt, "Man Against the Barren Grounds," 72.

3 Moffatt, "Man Against the Barren Grounds," 72.

4 Grinnell, *A Death on the Barrens*, 8.

5 Moffatt, "Danger and Sacrifice," 76.

6 Grinnell, *A Death on the Barrens*, 114–115.

7 Moffatt, "Part II: Man Against the Barren Grounds," 82.

8 Grinnell, *A Death on the Barrens*, 141.

9 Grinnell, *A Death on the Barrens*, 107.

CHAPTER 17

1 Back, *Narrative of the Arctic Land Expedition*, 205.
2 Back, *Narrative of the Arctic Land Expedition*, 220–221.

EPILOGUE

1 Kesselheim, "Moffatt Revisited," 52.
2 Steele, *The Man Who Mapped the Arctic*, 277.

BIBLIOGRAPHY

Back, George. *Narrative of the Arctic Land Expedition to the Mouth of the Great Fish River, and Along the Shores of the Arctic Ocean, in the Years 1833, 1834, and 1835*. New York: Elibron Classics, 2005.

Ballard, Carroll. *Never Cry Wolf*, DVD. Directed by Carroll Ballard. Burbank, California: Walt Disney Pictures, 2000.

Beattie, Owen, and John Geiger. *Frozen in Time: The Fate of the Franklin Expedition*. Vancouver: Greystone Books, 1998.

Bennett, John, and Susan Rowley, eds. *Uqalurait: An Oral History of Nunavut*. Montreal: McGill-Queen's University Press, 2004.

Berton, Pierre. *The Arctic Grail: The Quest for the North West Passage and the North Pole, 1818–1909*. Toronto: Anchor Canada, 1988.

Choque, Charles. *Joseph Buliard: Fisher of Men From Franche-Comte to the Canadian North*. Churchill, Manitoba: R.C. Episcopal Corporation, 1987.

Cronon, William. "The Trouble with Wilderness; or, Getting Back to the Wrong Nature." In *Uncommon Ground: Rethinking the Human Place in Nature*, edited by William Cronon, 69-90. New York: W.W. Norton & Co., 1996.

Explore Nunavut. "Whale Cove." Accessed March 5, 2010. http://www.explorenunavut.com/whalecove.php.

Gould, Glenn. "The Idea of North." *Ideas*. Dir. Glenn Gould. Toronto, ON: CBC Radio, December 27, 1967.

Grinnell, George. *A Death on the Barrens: A True Story of Courage and Tragedy in the Canadian Arctic*. North Ferrisburg, Vermont: Heron Dance Press and Art Studio, 1996.

Hall, Alex M. *Discovering Eden: A Lifetime of Paddling Arctic Rivers.* Toronto: Key Porter Books, 2003.

Hay, Elizabeth. *Late Nights on Air.* Toronto: McClelland & Stewart, 2007.

Heuer, Karsten. *Being Caribou: Five Months on Foot with an Arctic Herd.* Toronto: McClelland & Stewart, 2006.

Houston, C. Stuart, ed. *Arctic Artist: The Journal and Paintings of George Back, Midshipman with Franklin, 1819–1822.* Montreal: McGill-Queen's University Press, 1994.

——. *To the Arctic by Canoe 1819-1821: The Journal and Paintings of Robert Hood, Midshipman with Franklin.* Montreal: McGill-Queen's University Press, 1974.

Irvin, Tim, ed. *Arctic Inspired: A Tribute to the Tundra.* Victoria: Tundra Press, 2009.

——. "Stick with the Facts." *Kanawa Magazine* (Winter 2005/2006): 7.

Jacobs, Allan, October 24, 2008. "Back River, 2005," *Canadian Canoe Routes.* accessed March 15, 2014, http://www.myccr.com/phpbbforum/viewtopic.php?f=126&t=31348&start=0.

Kerasote, Ted. *Out There: In the Wild in a Wired Age.* Stillwater, Minnesota: Voyageur Press, 2004.

Kesselheim, Alan. "Moffatt Revisited." *Canoe & Kayak* (May 2012): 46–52, 102–103.

——. *The Wilderness Paddler's Handbook.* Toronto: McClelland & Stewart, Ltd., 2001.

King, Thomas. *The Truth About Stories: A Native Narrative.* Toronto: House of Anansi Press, 2003.

Kolbert, Elizabeth, ed. *The Arctic, An Anthology: Essential Readings on the Polar Region and its Future.* London: Granta Books, 2008.

Layman, Bill. "The $100,000 Rescue: Redux Potential Bowlers on the River Once More." *Kanawa Magazine* (Fall 2005): 19.

——. "The $100,000 Rescue: When Personal Locator Beacons Do—and Don't—Make Sense." *Kanawa Magazine* (Fall 2002): 34-37.

Leach, David. *Fatal Tide: When the Race of a Lifetime Goes Wrong.* Toronto: Viking Canada, 2008.

Lentz, John. "Expedition: Lookin' Back," *Che-mun,* accessed October 27, 2009, http://www.canoe.ca/che-mun/100back.html.

——. "Expedition: Lookin' Back Part II," *Che-mun,* accessed October 27, 2009, http://www.canoe.ca/che-mun/101back.html.

Lilburn, Tim. *Going Home.* Toronto: House of Anansi Press, 2008.

Lopez, Barry. *Arctic Dreams: Imagination and Desire in a Northern Landscape.* Toronto: Bantam Books, 1987.

McGhee, Robert. *Ancient People of the Arctic*. Vancouver: UBC Press, 1996.

Moffatt, Arthur, R. "Danger and Sacrifice." *Sports Illustrated,* March 16, 1959, accessed March 5, 2010, http://sportsillustrated.cnn.com/vault/article/magazine/MAG1070331/index.htm

——. "Man Against the Barren Grounds." *Sports Illustrated*, March 9, 1959, accessed March 5, 2010, http://sportsillustrated.cnn.com/vault/article/magazine/MAG1070294/index.htm.

Naughton, Donna. *The Natural History of Canadian Mammals*. Toronto: University of Toronto Press, 2012.

Pelly, David F. "The Mysterious Disappearance of Father Buliard, o.m.i." *Above & Beyond: Canada's Arctic Journal* (July/August 2005): 29–34.

Perkins, Robert. *Into the Great Solitude: An Arctic Journey*. New York: Dell Publishing, 1991.

Phillips, R.A.J. and G.F. Parsons. *This is the Arctic*. Ottawa: Department of Northern Affairs and National Resources, 1958.

Pick, Alison. "Paddling Back in Time," *The Walrus,* November 2007, accessed September 8, 2013, http://thewalrus.ca/2007-11-travel/.

——. *The Sweet Edge*. Vancouver: Raincoast Books, 2005.

Pielou, E.C. *A Naturalist's Guide to the Arctic*. Chicago: University of Chicago Press, 1994.

Purdy, Alfred. *North of Summer; Poems from Baffin Island*. Toronto: McClelland and Stewart, 1967.

Raffan, James. *Deep Waters: Is Adventure Worth the Risk: The Lake Timiskaming Canoeing Tragedy*. Toronto: Harper Perennial, 2002.

——. *Summer North of Sixty: By Paddle and Portage Across the Barren Lands*. Toronto: Key Porter Books, 1990.

Sibley, David Allen. *The Sibley Guide to Birds*. New York: Alfred A. Knopf, 2000.

——. *The Sibley Guide to Bird Life and Behavior*. New York: Alfred A. Knopf, 2001.

Steele, Peter. *The Man Who Mapped the Arctic: The Intrepid Life of George Back, Franklin's Lieutenant*. Vancouver: Raincoast Books, 2003.

Tester, Frank James, and Peter Kulchyski. *Tammarniit (Mistakes): Inuit Relocation in the Eastern Arctic, 1939-63*. Vancouver: UBC Press, 1994.

Thorpe, Natasha, et al. *Thunder on the Tundra: Inuit Quajimajatuqangit of the Bathurst Caribou*. Vancouver: Douglas and McIntyre, 2001.

Tranströmer, Tomas. "Guard Duty." In *Selected Poems*, edited by Robert Hass, 111–112. Hopewell, New Jersey: The Ecco Press, 1987.

Van Peenan, Paul. "A More Recent Look Back," *Che-mun,* accessed October 27, 2009, http://www.canoe.ca/che-mun/100back2.html.

Wiebe, Rudy. *A Discovery of Strangers*. Toronto: Knopf Canada, 1995.

THE DAVID SUZUKI FOUNDATION

THE DAVID SUZUKI Foundation works through science and education to protect the diversity of nature and our quality of life, now and for the future.

With a goal of achieving sustainability within a generation, the Foundation collaborates with scientists, business and industry, academia, government and non-governmental organizations. We seek the best research to provide innovative solutions that will help build a clean, competitive economy that does not threaten the natural services that support all life.

The Foundation is a federally registered independent charity that is supported with the help of over 50,000 individual donors across Canada and around the world.

We invite you to become a member. For more information on how you can support our work, please contact us:

The David Suzuki Foundation
219–2211 West 4th Avenue
Vancouver, BC
Canada v6k 4s2
www.davidsuzuki.org
contact@davidsuzuki.org
Tel: 604-732-4228
Fax: 604-732-0752

Checks can be made payable to the David Suzuki Foundation. All donations are tax-deductible.

Canadian charitable registration: (BN) 12775 6716 rr0001
U.S. charitable registration: #94-3204049